The Future of Catholic Theological Ethics

Special Issue Editor
Anna Abram

MDPI • Basel • Beijing • Wuhan • Barcelona • Belgrade

Special Issue Editor
Anna Abram
University of London
UK

Editorial Office
MDPI AG
St. Alban-Anlage 66
Basel, Switzerland

This edition is a reprint of the Special Issue published online in the open access journal *Religions* (ISSN 2077-1444) from 2017–2018 (available at: http://www.mdpi.com/journal/religions/special_issues/ethics).

For citation purposes, cite each article independently as indicated on the article page online and as indicated below:

Lastname, F.M.; Lastname, F.M. Article title. *Journal Name.* **Year**. *Article number, page range.*

First Edition 2018

ISBN 978-3-03842-771-1 (Pbk)
ISBN 978-3-03842-772-8 (PDF)

Articles in this volume are Open Access and distributed under the Creative Commons Attribution license (CC BY), which allows users to download, copy and build upon published articles even for commercial purposes, as long as the author and publisher are properly credited, which ensures maximum dissemination and a wider impact of our publications. The book taken as a whole is © 2018 MDPI, Basel, Switzerland, distributed under the terms and conditions of the Creative Commons license CC BY-NC-ND (http://creativecommons.org/licenses/by-nc-nd/4.0/).

Table of Contents

About the Special Issue Editor v

Preface to "The Future of Catholic Theological Ethics" vii

Anna Abram
Introduction to the Special Issue of Religions—The Future of Catholic Theological Ethics
doi: 10.3390/rel9010019 1

Joseph A. Selling
Reframing Catholic Theological Ethics: Summary and Application
doi: 10.3390/rel8100203 5

Lisa Sowle Cahill
Reframing Catholic Ethics: Is the Person an Integral and Adequate Starting Point?
doi: 10.3390/rel8100215 14

Mathew Illathuparampil
Goal-Oriented Ethics: Framing the Goal-Setting Concretely
doi: 10.3390/rel8100228 21

Mary Catherine OReilly-Gindhart
Pope Francis and Joseph Selling: A New Approach to Mercy in Catholic Sexual Ethics
doi: 10.3390/rel8120264 28

Nicholas Austin
Normative Virtue Theory in Theological Ethics
doi: 10.3390/rel8100211 37

Nenad Polgar
Reframing Catholic Theological Ethics from a Scotistic Perspective
doi: 10.3390/rel8100200 46

Jacqueline Stewart
Hermeneutic and Teleology in Ethics across Denominations—Thomas Aquinas and Karl Barth
doi: 10.3390/rel8100207 56

Peter Sedgwick
Anglican Moral Theology and Ecumenical Dialogue
doi: 10.3390/rel8090199 63

Marian Machinek
My Conscience is Clear (1 Cor 4:4). The Potential Relevance of Pauls Understanding of Conscience for Todays Fundamental Moral Theology
doi: 10.3390/rel8100201 71

Edward Vacek
Theocentric Love Ethics
doi: 10.3390/rel8100224 78

About the Special Issue Editor

Anna Abram was born in Poland where she studied theology and ethics. For 25 years she was at Heythrop College, University of London, where she completed her doctorate on the topic of moral development, taught ethics and worked as Head of Pastoral and Social Studies Department. She is Principal of the Margaret Beaufort Institute of Theology in Cambridge, UK. Most recently she co-edited a book (together with Peter Gallagher SJ and Michael Kirwan SJ) 'Philosophy, Theology and the Jesuit Tradition: The Eye of Love (T&T Clark/Bloomsbury, 2017) and was a guest editor of the Special Issue of 'Religions'(2017) entitled 'The Future of Catholic Theological Ethics'. She co-edits (together with Janusz Salamon) a book series 'Bloomsbury Studies in Global Ethics'.

Preface to "The Future of Catholic Theological Ethics"

This special issue of *Religions* considers the question of the future of Catholic Theological Ethics. It recognises the moral wisdom of the past and searches for new ways of making Catholic theological ethics pertinent. The papers presented here cover several major themes that, traditionally, Catholic theological ethics have considered but, according to the authors of the papers, need revisiting. Each contribution engages with the publication *Reframing Catholic Theological Ethics* (Oxford University Press, 2016) by Joseph Selling, Emeritus Professor of Moral Theology, Catholic University Leuven. The collection explores such themes as conscience, virtue, natural law, authority, ecumenism, the human person and the theology of theological ethics. The writers represent a variety of approaches, geographical locations (Western and Eastern Europe, USA, and India) and while most of them are Roman Catholic, there is an imbedded ecumenism as well as interreligious and inter-cultural slant in several papers. I hope that this collection will ignite a lively debate about the future of Catholic Theological Ethics and you, the reader, will make it radiate further.

Anna Abram
Special Issue Editor

Editorial

Introduction to the Special Issue of Religions—"The Future of Catholic Theological Ethics"

Anna Abram

The Margaret Beaufort Institute of Theology, 12 Grange Road, Cambridge CB3 9DU, UK; aa2008@cam.ac.uk

Received: 7 December 2017; Accepted: 19 December 2017; Published: 10 January 2018

If the past is said to be a foreign country, then the future must be even less native. This is something many Catholic theological ethicists feel when they look back into the history of moral theological reflection and attempt to relate it to practical issues of today. What should be the starting point for discussing the future of Catholic Theological Ethics? It is not easy to address this question at the time of unprecedented change in which political upheavals, migration of people, inequalities, climate change, views on gender, sexuality, human relationality (including the relationality of the human to the non-human species) are amongst many issues that require careful attention and new understanding. This is in no way to imply that what went on before in Catholic ethics is no longer relevant. Arguably, the moral wisdom of the tradition is an important resource. However, new approaches, both theoretical and practical, are needed. The ten contributors to this special issue of *Religions* search for new ways of making Catholic theological ethics pertinent. For each of them the starting point of discussion is the groundbreaking publication *Reframing Catholic Theological Ethics* (Oxford University Press, 2016) by Joseph Selling, Emeritus Professor of Moral Theology, Catholic University Leuven.

The papers presented here cover several major themes that, traditionally, Catholic theological ethics have considered but, according to the authors of the papers, need revisiting. Amongst these themes are: conscience, virtue, natural law, authority, ecumenism, the human person and the *theology* of theological ethics. The writers represent a variety of approaches, geographical locations (Western and Eastern Europe, USA, and India) and while most of them are Roman Catholic, there is an imbedded ecumenism in several discussions and there is a direct and indirect interreligious and inter-cultural slant in some of the papers.

Joseph Selling opens the issue with a summary of the approach he developed in the above-mentioned publication. In his 'Reframing Catholic Theological Ethics: Summary and Application' (Selling 2017) he argues that while traditional Catholic moral theology has much to offer regarding responsible, ethical living and decision-making, the method of theological ethics used over the centuries doesn't serve us well today. The aim of theological ethics in the past was to train priests for hearing confessions and helping them to judge whether acts confessed were sinful or not. Selling traces the history of the discourse and notes that while the goal of the acting person was also important in judging the acts, it was only in order to find whether the guilt of the penitent was possible to mitigate. Selling makes a case for inclusion in the method a proper attention to the goals of ethical living. He proposes a review of ethical terminology, especially the meaning of good, bad and evil. He builds his method of moral evaluation and decision-making on the work of Thomas Aquinas and the documents of the Second Vatican Council which urged the adaptation of a norm broadly called as 'Human Person Integrally and Adequately Considered'. He offers a new reading of 'circumstances', 'ends' and 'intentions' as well as virtues. He lists twenty 'principles' which for him are part and parcel of the Catholic ethical tradition: 'the need for a working *anthropology*, an emphasis on *attitude* before behavior, a sense of *commitment* to life projects, protecting the *common good*, maintaining a sense of *community*, validation of *corporeality*, striving toward *detachment*, fostering love of *enemies* protecting our *environment*, promoting *equal human* dignity, maintaining an *eschatological* sense, construction of a shared *ethics*, belief in basic *goodness*, cultivating a sense of *justice*, communicating through *narrative*, embracing an *option* for the disadvantaged, seeking *reconciliation* whenever possible, exercising *responsibility*, recognizing the reality of sin developing a life of *virtue*'. Selling considers a number of challenges for the future Catholic theological ethics including, at the end of his paper here and the book, the challenge of teaching.

Lisa Sowle Cahill (Cahill 2017) in her 'Reframing Catholic Ethics: Is the Person an Integral and Adequate Starting Point?' explores a different type of challenge (although with the implication on teaching): the person as the starting point for ethical reflection. While making a response to Selling's method of moral evaluation and using the example of the HIV/AIDS problem (introduced by Selling), Cahill challenges the Western tendency to view the human person as a free and responsible moral agent. She calls for a more social, inductive, and global approach in which a greater attention is given to the social and political aspects of sex and gender and to the intersection of gender, race, class and economic inequality. Cahill is interested in the way non-Western perspectives might inform and alter Western methods and conclusions. She not only expands certain aspects of Selling's perspective but makes a strong case for a cross-communal and dialogic ethics, which is appreciative of what we (as human beings) share and how we differ.

Another challenge, namely a challenge to concretize goal-oriented moral thinking, is explored by Illathuparampil (Illathuparampil 2017) and Marie Catherine O'Reilly-Gindhart (O'Reilly-Gindhart 2017). Illathuparampil in his 'Goal-Oriented Ethics: Framing the Goal-Setting Concretely' discusses 'four supportive pillars' which aim to supplement Selling's approach: (1) openness to human sciences; (2) conversation among various narratives; (3) positing a theological frame for ethical reasoning; (4) recourse to non-discursive reasoning. O'Reilly-Gindhard in her 'Pope Francis and Joseph Selling: A New Approach to Mercy in Catholic Sexual Ethics', uses Selling's method of the 'virtuous trapezium' to analyse Pope Francis's approach to matters concerning sexuality in his Apostolic Exhortation of *Amoris Laetitia* (Franciscus 2016a) and Apostolic Letter *Misericordia et Misera* (Franciscus 2016b). She finds a number of interesting connections between Pope Francis and Selling and shows how the insights of the two could advance our understanding of the virtue of mercy.

Nicholas Austin (Austin 2017) in his 'Normative Virtue Theory in Theological Ethics' supports Selling's turn to virtue. However, Austin is aware that many theological ethicists dismiss virtue theory and see it as normatively weak. So, prior to endorsing Selling's turn to virtue, Austin considers the key objections to the normativity of virtue theory and responds to them by drawing on Thomas Aquinas and contemporary discussions. He makes a strong case that virtue theory is about qualities of character that are oriented towards action; virtue theory provides a rich moral vocabulary for describing moral rightness or wrongness of actions and offers the right level of normative guidance. Austin wants future theological ethics to 'reap the benefits of the renewal of virtue by recognising that virtue theory is normative'.

Nenad Polgar (Polgar 2017) in his 'Reframing Catholic Theological Ethics from a Scotistic Perspective' responds to Selling's invitation to re-think the post-Tridentine development of theological ethics but unlike Selling (and Austin) Polgar doesn't find the Thomistic approach helpful. According to him, one of the problems is the unresolved debate within the discipline on how Aquinas' texts ought to be interpreted. So, Polgar proposes an alternative route via the (presumably, less ambiguous) works of John Duns Scotus. He reflects on Scotus' study of marriage and bigamy in the Old Testament that, in Polgar's view, justifies drawing a parallel between Scotus' work and Selling's attempt to reframe Catholic theological ethics.

The exercise of reframing Catholic theological ethics into a more ecumenical discourse is considered by Stewart (Stewart 2017) in her 'Hermeneutic and teleology in ethics across denominations—Thomas Aquinas and Karl Barth' and Peter Sedgwick in his 'Anglican moral theology and ecumenical dialogue' (Sedgwick 2017). Stewart's study arises from the context of current debates in the Catholic Church on the place of rule and law in moral reasoning. She suggests that ethics may be best served by approaches that place the human subject in a teleological context and that recognise the need for interpretation of circumstances surrounding actions to be evaluated. As several authors mentioned above, Stewart too supports a contextualized approach to theological ethics and contrasts it with normative rule approaches. She compares Selling's insights on moral reasoning in Aquinas with an account of the ethical implications in Karl Barth's theology of hope as expressed in Volume Four of the *Church Dogmatics* (Barth 1967). Stewart concludes that, in an ecumenical convergence, neither propose a normative rule approach. Rather both use a teleological context and require a hermeneutic of evaluation. Sedgwick, an Anglican moral theologian, advances three ecumenically relevant arguments: (1) Roman Catholic moral theology has been in a state of sustained engagement, and sometimes outright conflict on the nature of moral theology and the place of the human agent, since the 1960s; (2) this debate has overshadowed the search for ecumenical rapprochement in many places, but especially the acceptance of the report on moral theology entitled Life in Christ from the Anglican—Roman Catholic International Commission (ARCIC); (3) Sedgwick suggests that there are contributions which Anglican ethics can bring both to the Catholic debate, and to ecumenism, in the area of moral norms and the nature of a moral absolute. He substantiates these contributions by exploring the works of Richard Hooker, Jeremy Taylor, and Kenneth Kirk. Sedgwick pays attention to something that is also important to Selling, namely the theology of theological ethics, a theme which the final two papers address more directly: the theocentric study of conscience in St Paul by Marian Machinek and love ethics by Edward Vacek.

Machinek (2017) in his 'My conscience is clear' (1 Cor 4:4) examines the Pauline understanding of conscience while aiming to formulate some of the foundations of the Christian ethics. Machinek argues that the meaning Paul attaches to conscience depends on the context (mainly in Rom and 1–2 Cor), ranging from the personal to the communal one. He finds an important inspiration in the way Paul considers the relationship between various members of the *ecclesia*: those appointed to hold authority and those who supposed to submit to it. He suggests that despite the variety of differences between our and Paul's worlds, Paul offers important insights on the foundations of Christian ethics, especially in ensuring that the foundations remain theological. Vacek's (Vacek 2017) study of 'Theocentric Love Ethics' is committed to the theological turn in ethics. He acknowledges and even endorses contemporary attempts to revise natural law ethics by turning towards a more theocentric approach in theological ethics. He goes even further by proposing his own love-covenant approach. Vacek contrasts secular and religious ethics. Religious ethics, for him, involves communion with God. As several other contributors to this issue, he builds his position on Thomas Aquinas.

It seems that one of most important services that Catholic theological ethicists could offer to contemporary debates on pressing moral issues is to help others to discern. Vacek sees discernment as an affective process of union with God. When talking about this union he warns against the dangers of the reductionist view of this union in which God is reduced to self or self to God. This is an important warning to bear in mind, especially as theological ethicists find themselves in increasingly less 'native' lands or less familiar territories and prepare themselves for greater inter-denominational, inter-religious, inter-cultural, and inter-disciplinary engagements. As the papers presented here suggest, for Catholic theological ethics to be relevant it has to become more context-sensitive, ecumenical, practice-based, experience-oriented, continuously discerning, pedagogically wide-ranging and theologically articulate. It has to be unceasingly willing to review and renew its method as well as revisit its key concepts. It must neither dismiss its long tradition nor stick to its single interpretation.

Conflicts of Interest: The author declares no conflict of interest.

References

Austin, Nicholas. 2017. Normative Virtue Theory in Theological Ethics. *Religions* 8: 211. [CrossRef]
Barth, Karl. 1967. *Church Dogmatics*. Translated by G. W. Bromiley. Edited by G. W. Bromiley and T. F. Torrance. Edinburgh: T & T Clark.
Cahill, Lisa Sowle. 2017. Reframing Catholic Ethics: Is the Person an Integral and Adequate Starting Point? *Religions* 8: 215. [CrossRef]

Franciscus, I. 2016a. Amoris Laetitia, Post-Synodal Exhortation. March 19. Available online: https://w2.vatican.va/content/dam/francesco/pdf/apost_exhortations/documents/papa-francesco_esortazione-ap_20160319_amoris-laetitia_en.pdf (accessed on 16 June 2017).

Franciscus, I. 2016b. Misericordia Et Misera. November 20. Available online: https://w2.vatican.va/content/francesco/en/apost_letters/documents/papa-francesco-lettera-ap_20161120_misericordia-et-misera.html (accessed on 16 June 2017).

Illathuparampil, Mathew. 2017. Goal-Oriented Ethics: Framing the Goal-Setting Concretely. *Religions* 8: 228. [CrossRef]

Machinek, Marian. 2017. "My Conscience is Clear" (1 Cor 4:4). The Potential Relevance of Paul's Understanding of Conscience for Today's Fundamental Moral Theology. *Religions* 8: 201. [CrossRef]

O'Reilly-Gindhart, Mary Catherine. 2017. Pope Francis and Joseph Selling: A New Approach to Mercy in Catholic Sexual Ethics. *Religions* 8: 264. [CrossRef]

Polgar, Nenad. 2017. Reframing Catholic Theological Ethics from a Scotistic Perspective. *Religions* 8: 200. [CrossRef]

Sedgwick, Peter. 2017. Anglican Moral Theology and Ecumenical Dialogue. *Religions* 8: 199. [CrossRef]

Selling, Joseph A. 2017. Reframing Catholic Theological Ethics: Summary and Application. *Religions* 8: 203. [CrossRef]

Stewart, Jacqueline. 2017. Hermeneutic and Teleology in Ethics across Denominations—Thomas Aquinas and Karl Barth. *Religions* 8: 207. [CrossRef]

Vacek, Edward. 2017. Theocentric Love Ethics. *Religions* 8: 224. [CrossRef]

© 2018 by the author. Licensee MDPI, Basel, Switzerland. This article is an open access article distributed under the terms and conditions of the Creative Commons Attribution (CC BY) license (http://creativecommons.org/licenses/by/4.0/).

Article

Reframing Catholic Theological Ethics: Summary and Application

Joseph A. Selling

Research Unit of Theological and Comparative Ethics, Katholieke Universiteit Leuven, Leuven 3000, Belgium; joseph.selling@kuleuven.be

Received: 21 August 2017; Accepted: 20 September 2017; Published: 25 September 2017

Abstract: This text represents a summary of the major points developed in the book, *Reframing Catholic Theological Ethics*, and a brief overview of how the author understands the relation between religion, ethics, and the building of a virtuous community. The main points of the book involve the anatomy of "the moral event" that includes a breakdown of all the elements necessary to consider before one arrives at ethical judgments and decision-making. Foundations are brought forth for these elements, each of which exhibits its own characteristics. The good and evil details of actions and circumstances that make up behavior are based upon an analysis of what is beneficial or harmful to human persons, integrally and adequately considered. Behaviors themselves are considered right or wrong in relation to whether they are appropriate ways of achieving one's intended ends. Then, the distinction between good and bad is related to one's virtuous or vicious dispositions, which necessitates a revised understanding of virtue. Based upon a view of religion that provides a formulation of principles that guide the life of the believing community, it is suggested that these principles encourage a commitment to ends or goals that serve the maintenance and advance of a community's ethics.

Keywords: ethics; intention; virtue; principles; narrative

In March 2016, I published *Reframing Catholic Theological Ethics* (Selling 2016). A major premise of this study is that traditional Catholic moral theology was fashioned not to point the way toward responsible, ethical living and decision-making, but rather to train priests how to hear confessions. As a result, the emphasis of the discipline fell upon the actions and omissions that were reported by penitents and which the priest-confessor had to judge as sinful or not, as gravely sinful or less so.

The early (from the seventh century) penitential books listed sins by describing acts (or omissions) along with any circumstances that might have a bearing on their offensiveness. These behaviors were evaluated in themselves with little attention being given to the motive or intention of the person who performed them. The moral theological textbooks that developed as a result of the counter-reformation (in the sixteenth century) followed along these lines, although they attempted to incorporate some theoretical basis for the teaching presented. This included some account of conscience which was usually described as the capacity or mechanism for appropriating moral laws and applying them to concrete situations. In this tradition, the end or goal of the acting person was considered important, but only in the sense of establishing or mitigating the guilt of the penitent. It had no bearing on the evaluation of individual behaviors.

We have learned from modern psychology that healthy, adult, and attentive persons do not choose behaviors in a random manner (Maslow [1954] 1987). Although they may be attracted to certain behaviors emotionally, mature persons develop the capacity to weigh short-term satisfactions against long-term accomplishments and subsequent satisfaction. The ends or goals of ethical living are important with respect to making ethical decisions (Rokeach 1973). Further, in a very real way, they form the starting point of that decision-making. Aiming at more long-term goals helps to clarify how to arrange and prioritize short-term goals in order to facilitate making choices about what to do (or omit). These short-term ends or goals are the object of the person's ethical intention. In schematic form (see Figure 1).

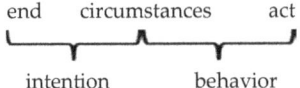

Figure 1. The sources of morality (expanded).

Neither ends nor actions on their own can determine an ethical evaluation outside of a context of circumstances. One could imagine several ends toward which a person might aim. But one could only ethically commit to the realization of a specific end or goal within circumstances that provide a minimum of opportunity for achieving that end. When this occurs, one may—or may not—formulate an intention to achieve that end.

By the same token, one could consider a range of options for achieving one's ends. But ethically choosing which of these options one might implement depends upon the presence of a given set of circumstances. Performing actions within those circumstances constitutes a behavior. Behaviors can be very different even when the action performed is exactly the same. Striking a person may represent camaraderie, insult, offense, or self-defense. Killing a person may represent punishment, personal hatred, defense of an innocent party, or simply an accident.

1. Expansion and Precision of Ethical Terminology

Traditionally, textbook moral theology presented "the moral act" as a phenomenon that could be assessed by considering the so-called "sources of morality". These sources consisted in the act itself, the consequences surrounding that act, and the end or intention of the acting person. This classical paradigm suffered from a fundamental ambiguity because it was not always clear what one meant by the word "act": was it referring to the entire event or simply to the performance of a material action (or omission)? When moral theologians refer to "acts" that are "evil in themselves" they beg more questions than they answer, none of which contribute to ethical insight.

By making distinctions between intentions and ends, and between acts and behaviors, we introduce both nuance and precision into our ethical vocabulary. Each of the elements presented here can be examined on their own. They are distinct. However, when they all work together, they form a unity, a single, complex phenomenon that I refer to as a "moral event".

I will examine the meaning of these terms shortly (see Figure 2), but first I would like to point out that, when using the terms in an ethical context, each one of them is subject to (a somewhat different form of) evaluation. Fortunately, the English language provides us with different words to describe the kind of evaluation that is taking place.

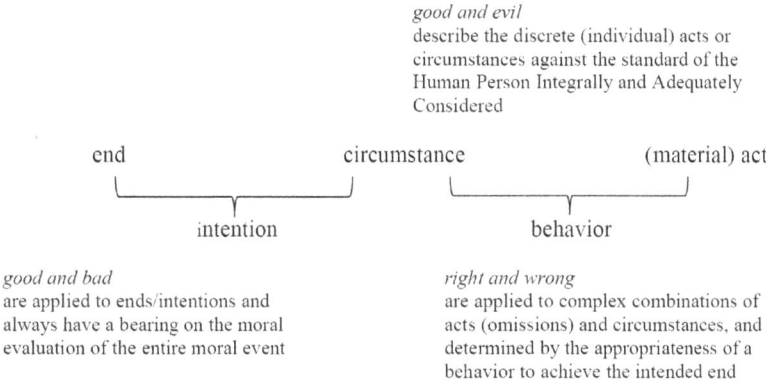

Figure 2. The moral event.

In English, the word "good" has two possible antonyms, evil and bad. This allows us to assign each word-pair to a different form of evaluation. One could be used in an expressly moral[1] context, while the other can be used as a descriptive term, indicating its morally relevant characteristics but stopping short of making a moral judgment.

Most of us would agree that if the intention of the acting person is not good, the entirety of the moral event will be corrupt and cannot be made good, no matter how much beneficence flows from it. The classic example here is giving to charity in order to gain the admiration of others. Therefore, I would assign the word-pair good and bad to label the ethical character of one's intention-to-an-end.

On the other hand, the discrete elements of material actions and the circumstances that influence their morally relevant characteristics are descriptive and not (yet) morally qualified. Imprisoning a person, for instance, may be described as an evil—something disadvantageous for the person being imprisoned—and the circumstance that the duration of imprisonment is for the remainder of their life adds another dimension of disadvantage which is also negative in character. Nevertheless, there may be other circumstances, such as who this person is and what they may have done in the past, that make the evil(s) of the action (behavior) justifiable as punishment.

Behaviors represent the decided-upon combination of actions and circumstances that the person may ultimately choose in order to achieve their intended end. They are classified as "right or wrong" depending upon two factors: whether this choice of behavior has a reasonable chance to accomplish the intended end, and whether the evil(s) associated with this behavior neither contradict nor overshadow the good that is being achieved through the moral event. This, of course, is a matter of prudential judgment.

2. Acts and Circumstances: The Meaning of Good and Evil

When Thomas Aquinas described the circumstances surrounding human moral (voluntary) activity (S.T., I-II, q. 7, a. 3), following Cicero he lists them as who, what, where, by what aids, why, how, when, and, following Aristotle, about what. Note that the "what" (I take something belonging to another) and the "about what" (I take a little or a lot, from the poor or the rich, etc.) are listed as *circumstances*. They do not constitute a "human act" because an "activity" can only be considered human when it is voluntary, when it proceeds from the will that is first manifest in the activity called

---

[1] I use the word "moral" (antonym: immoral) here because this linguistic category is clearly judgmental in tone. The word "ethical" is primarily used to describe the type of discourse that is taking place. Its antithetical counterpart, unethical, can hardly be used to describe things like murder, rape, or torture.

intention ("the end is last in execution, but first in the intention of reason, according to which moral actions receive their species", q. 18, a. 7, ad 2).

In the following article (q. 7, a. 4), Aquinas tells us that the two circumstances, why and what, are the most important. The reason that the circumstance "why" is important is because it describes "the motive and the object of the will which is the end". A truly human act must be voluntary, and the will to the end (intention) is what motivates the moral event in the first place. That said, although a bad intention will corrupt a moral event "from the beginning", on its own a good intention cannot guarantee that the moral event will be a good one.

What is done is also important because, without something "being done", the end will never be achieved. Again, although the thing done along with all the relevant circumstances can be judged to be right or wrong, purely on its own, the behavior cannot determine the status of the moral event without taking into account the intention to the end of the acting person and the freedom present in the will when choosing. The choice of a wrong behavior could be the result of ignorance.

Responding to the question about how one assigns the labels "good and evil" to the *circumstances* of what is done, textbook moral theology would search for a "ruling" on that matter either from a stipulation found in the scriptures or from its own attempt to analyze a "natural law". Neither of these, however, is adequate for the task. Even clear commandments, such as "thou shalt not kill" admit of exceptions that have been enshrined in church teaching for centuries. And what is considered to be "against nature" can turn out to be largely beneficial for human persons. (At the beginning of the nineteenth century, for instance, many looked upon the technique of vaccination as working against the natural law.) Therefore, the documents of the Second Vatican Council urged the adaptation of a different norm for making these evaluations, namely the Human Person Integrally and Adequately Considered.

Far from understanding, the human person as a mere individual, the anthropology worked out by many moral theologians stresses the interconnectedness of persons that flows from the many dimensions of being human that are weaved together to form a realistic and integral notion of what it means to be human persons. An example of the multidimensionality of the human person was developed by Louis Janssens on the basis of the text of *Gaudium et spes* (Janssens 1980; Selling 1998).

1. Human Persons stand in relation to everything, to the whole of reality
2. Human Persons stand in relation to the material world
3. Human Persons are cultural
4. Human Persons are historical
5. Human Persons stand in particular relationships with other persons
6. Human Persons become a conscious interiority, a subject
7. Human Persons are corporeal subjects
8. Every Human Person is unique, yet fundamentally equal in dignity

Whatever protects, promotes, or enhances human persons can be understood as good: it is "good for persons". Whatever threatens, harms, or diminishes human persons can be understood as evil: it is "evil for persons". These goods and evils are morally relevant and an important part of one's ethical analysis of choosing a behavior. But they do not ipso facto determine the ethical evaluation of a complex moral event. For instance, the removal of an organ is an evil, but it can be justified when it protects the well-being of the whole body.

3. Ends and Intentions: The Meaning of Good and Bad

Attention to the circumstance "why" reveals the motivation of the acting person. Many people give insufficient consideration to this aspect of their ethical decision-making and end up pursuing short-term goals that distort their understanding of the challenge they may be facing. At least part of the reason why this happens is because traditional morality tended to focus on behaviors alone, without focusing on the larger picture. Attempts to consider ends or goals as the starting point of ethical discourse were linked to "consequentialism", a theory that suggests that it is *only* the outcome of our activity that matters in decision-making.

Fear of consequentialism led many moral theologians to disvalue or even ignore the outcome of ethical decision-making. They failed to see that consideration of the motive of the acting person, which can only be discerned through an examination of the end or goal that the person intends to accomplish, is an integral part of human voluntary activity. What motivates us reveals our ethical character and disposition. It is that disposition that helps us determine whether intention is good or bad. A good disposition is said to be virtuous, while a bad disposition is not virtuous and may even be vicious.

Most of us have accepted the idea that virtuous dispositions are learned. They are built up as habits of choosing a path that is virtuous[2]. By the same token, making vicious decisions leads to being habitually vicious in our outlook and therefore prone to intending ends or goals that exhibit that viciousness. But what are the virtues, exactly? The Catholic tradition has recognized three "theological virtues" from St. Paul's writings and four "cardinal virtues" inherited from ancient Greek philosophy. Some, like Aquinas, have attempted to break each of these down into more specific parts, but the framework of the seven categories remains limited. Perhaps this is the reason why virtue theory never became a significant part of the dynamics of doing theological ethics.

Another reason why virtue theory did not succeed in shedding light on the importance of one's intention-to-an-end in ethical evaluation is because virtues were treated as singular and static ideas. The classic idea that virtue stands as the mean between two extremes was virtually beyond question until Peter Knauer made a provocative suggestion for an alternative perspective.[3]

Referring to Aristotle's famous dictum about virtue standing between two extremes, as in bravery or courage being a "mean" between foolhardiness and cowardice, he observed that even "The Philosopher" noted that bravery is closer to the extreme of foolhardiness than it is to cowardice. Knauer then asked whether there was another virtue that was closer to the extreme of cowardice than it is to foolhardiness, and he suggested that there was indeed prudence, or as I would call it, caution. Giving five more examples of two virtues being relevant to a given challenge that could reciprocally moderate two extremes, Knauer referred to this as a square and claimed that it was a universal phenomenon. However, he then went on with his study without elaborating any further on how we could better understand the concept of virtue.

Because two virtues occupy the middle ground between two extremes of inappropriate attitudes, I prefer to use the schema of a trapezoid rather than a square (see Figure 3). I also refer to the two virtues as "complementary virtues" that describe a continuum within which the virtuous person would seek an appropriate solution to a given challenge by taking account of all the relevant details—circumstances—of a presenting issue. The issue calling forth the virtues of courage and caution can be described as facing up to a dangerous situation or perhaps even some form of opposition. The virtuous response that the person gives to the situation will depend upon several circumstances that could not be known before one actually confronts such a situation. What we do know is that one's response should lie somewhere on the continuum (signified by the dotted line in the diagram) between the two, complementary virtues. Total courage without any hint of caution would be foolhardiness. Total caution without any hint of courage would be cowardice. The "mean" being suggested by Aristotle is thus not an absolute point.

---

[2] Some virtues are such that they cannot be arrived at on one's own. The individual needs to be "given" reasons to have faith in the meaning of life, see hope that good will ultimately prevail, and receive compassion that demonstrates the meaning of love.

[3] Peter Knauer, "La Détermination du bien et du mal moral par le principe du double effet" (Knauer 1965, pp. 356–76). This was later published in a reworked version in English as "The Hermeneutic Function of the Principle of Double Effect" (Knauer 1967, pp. 132–62) and was reprinted in Charles E. Curran and Richard A. McCormick (eds.), *Moral Norms and Catholic Tradition* (Knauer 1979, here, pp. 1–39).

Figure 3. The Virtuous Trapezoid.

The elaboration of complementary virtues is, in my opinion, an ongoing project. One can begin by identifying ethically challenging situations and then ask what the possible virtues and vices (extremes) might be; conversely, one could look at a list of virtues and then identify the type of challenge to which it responds so that one can set the stage for identifying the complementary virtue that, together with the first, holds the extremes in check. In the book, I identify 55 sets of complementary virtues that the reader can also find on my website.[4]

It also bears observing that virtues are not necessarily eternal or transcultural. Although some of the virtues such as kindness, hope, and patience occupy a hallowed place in most societies, others are more culturally connected in their expression, such as modesty, discretion, and industriousness. Some virtues mentioned by medieval thinkers like Aquinas, such as magnanimity and magnificence, are no longer helpful, while others have only been recognized in recent times, such as stewardship, self-care, and ecumenism. Then there are some virtues, such as truthfulness and responsibility that receive widespread approval but rather dubious observance in many social settings.

4. Religion's Role in Emphasizing Attitudes

Most religions impress upon their adherents some code of conduct that approves, demands, or condemns various forms of behavior. Torah, for instance, stipulates 365 negative and 248 positive laws that rule just about every facet of life. Catholic Christianity deeply respects the tradition of Judaism, but does not subscribe to the vast majority of their laws. It explicitly teaches the Decalogue, but then presumes to elaborate ancillary meanings of the commandments worked out through a system of "natural law" reasoning. This is founded upon the presupposition that, since God is the author of creation, its "natural" structure and laws must be of divine origin and are therefore inviolable.

What we have too often allowed to escape our attention is that there is another approach to ethical reflection present in our Judeo-Christian tradition that addresses something other than normative stipulations. At the end of the second chapter of the book, I draw attention to twenty "principles" which I consider to be part and parcel of the Catholic ethical tradition. Eleven of these, I believe, can find substantiation in the scriptures. In the following paragraph, they are named with the italicized words.

> The People of God identify themselves as a *community*. Individuals may sometimes play a prominent role, but this is always understood to be in service to that community. Fleshing out the history, identity, and destiny of the community is achieved through *narrative*, the continuous story of the people and its individual members. Together, they seek *justice* by exercising *responsibility*. Thus, while affirming the fundamental *goodness* of persons and the community, as well as the whole creation, there remains a consciousness of the presence of *sin* that brings about disruption. This demands that they continuously seek *reconciliation* among all persons. Outside the community, this should even be extended to *enemies*. Included in this is the need to be sensitive to those who do not enjoy justice

---

[4] The four pages on the topic can be found at: https://perswww.kuleuven.be/~u0010542/theory/virtue.html. In the book, my tentative list of virtues and vices can be found in Appendix 9.

and therefore deserve the benefit of an *option* to respond to and restore their justifiable claims. The deeds that are called for to achieve all these goals will only be pursued when the people embrace a proper *attitude*, one that seeks righteousness not only in the present but also in the future, the hoped-for *eschatological* ideals that motivate the people.

Through the course of history, which when narrated as the unfolding of the message contained in the scriptures is referred to as tradition, we witness the community of believers recognizing that they need to adapt their social, cultural, and political practices to remain true to that message. In doing so, they formulate principles that they consider to flow from or be compatible with the narrative they are attempting to live out. Some of these are temporary, but others exhibit a lasting character that becomes integrated into the ethic of the community of believers, even institutionalized in the medium that we refer to as church. In the following paragraph, I point to nine principles that I believe reflect the ethics of the post-Vatican II church, although most of them pre-date that event. Again, they are named with the italicized words.

The idea of formulating and being motivated by principles leads toward the adaptation of a philosophical insight referred to as *virtue*, or the acquisition of habits that influence the way in which we respond to life's challenges. Virtues lead to the construction of a particular kind of *ethics* that not only reflects our understanding of scripture but also is grounded in our social and cultural experience. Because of its sense of community, the Catholic view of the world values what is referred to as the *common good*, a concept that needs to be continually updated in light of what we learn through the human sciences. This entails the development of a functional *anthropology* that, in many places of the world, is understood to include the *equal dignity* of all human persons, regardless of gender, skin color, ethnic affiliation, and so forth. At the same time, we must admit that our Catholic Christian tradition has had difficulty coming to terms with human *corporeality*, especially sexuality, something that should be appreciated in a virtuous manner. Then, with regard to material things we are aware of a definite strain in our tradition that values *detachment*. While some will claim that a sense of *commitment* has always been part of the Christian tradition, this has usually been thought of in absolute terms, whereas there is a necessary place for short-term commitment as well, especially in terms of evolving life projects. Finally, it has only been in the last sixty or seventy years that we have developed a sense of responsibility in caring for the *environment*.

These twenty principles describe the contours of ethical living and decision-making. They lead us to articulating the meaning of virtue that in turn motivates us to identify goals to be accomplished in life, both as a community and as individuals. However, this is an on-going process that, for the individual, spans an entire lifetime.

In the table below (see Table 1), I list the principles in alphabetical order in order to dispel the impression of a hierarchy of importance. I believe that the character of Catholic Christian ethics demands attention to these principles, which in turn should inspire individuals to shape their attitudes and thus their habitual responses to their community and their environment. I do not consider this list to be either complete or fully accurate, but I offer it as a focal point of further discussion.

Table 1. General principles of Catholic Christian ethics.

Scripture	General Principles	Tradition
attitude community enemies eschatological goodness justice narrative option reconciliation responsibility sin	the need for a working *anthropology* an emphasis on *attitude* before behavior a sense of *commitment* to life projects protecting the *common good* maintaining a sense of *community* validation of *corporeality* striving toward *detachment* fostering love of *enemies* protecting our *environment* promoting *equal human dignity* maintaining an *eschatological* sense construction of a shared *ethics* belief in basic *goodness* cultivating a sense of *justice* communicating through *narrative* embracing an *option* for the disadvantaged seeking *reconciliation* whenever possible exercising *responsibility* recognizing the reality of *sin* developing a life of *virtue*	anthropology commitment common good corporeality detachment environment equal dignity ethicsvirtue virtue

By developing and promoting these principles, religion, or similar systems of belief, stimulates the motivational aspects of what it means to be a member of that describable community of persons. General motivations lead to the formation of attitudes that influence goal orientation and the intentions to achieve those goals or ends. Motivations simultaneously predispose individuals to give attention to the expectations of the community that are embodied in normative ethics. However, beginning from the perspective of personal responsibility and the formation of intentions, norms and laws will be understood in their supportive and educative function rather than as behavioral dictates.

5. The Challenge of Teaching

If we adapt an intentional, attitudinal approach to ethical living and decision-making, we will have to accept the fact that the way we teach this—both to children and to the community of adults who share our belief system—will have to be different from simply listing rules or laws to be followed. With young people, this clearly cannot begin until they reach a reasonable age for understanding the importance of building character. However, if the adults responsible for their education already understand and are practicing such an ethical approach, this will influence the ethical education of those in their charge. Knowing, and especially articulating, the underlying principles and motivations that inspire ethical behavior will help avoid the impression that rules should be followed simply because they are imposed by authority.

One of the general principles listed above points to the importance of *narrative* in the way that we communicate our beliefs. Considering that an ethical system is based upon what we believe about ourselves, our communities, and our world, we need to articulate and seek a consensus about that narrative. This would reflect the teaching of Jesus through his words and deeds. However, before we fall into the trap of reading our own meaning into the scriptures, we need to study them and to seek out competent persons to explain them and their context. Each community will have its particular perspective on what the stories relate.

For instance, those who live in a political dictatorship will likely emphasize certain parts of the scriptures while those living in a liberal democracy will emphasize other parts. This is a task that needs to be shared by all the members of a community, being attentive to the different aspects of how life is experienced and represented. Relevant social, economic, ethnic, and historical factors should all be considered. At the same time, this coming together needs to be guided not only by experts (theologians) but also by those who provide spiritual advice (religious), and those who maintain a link to the world church (bishops).

Before we turn in on ourselves and mistake the source of ethical insight to lie exclusively within our own tradition, we should recognize that (ethical) narratives are all around us. Story-telling, literature, motion pictures, television programs, and even the way that news items are sometimes presented, offer a narrative that invites ethical analysis. The story does not have to be of our own making to be a worthy vehicle for learning or providing role models. Christianity has infiltrated just about every culture on the face of the earth, sometimes disrupting it but also learning from it and adapting ethically relevant principles. Think, for instance, about the human rights tradition that the European churches resisted for so long, before recognizing it as nearly perfectly compatible with the teaching of the New Testament.

Further, one of the sub-principles of the social teaching of the church is the principle of subsidiarity, whereby challenges need to be faced and resolved at the presenting level and not from the outside or "on high". When this is followed, the global community of the church will see the emergence of different ways of dealing with similar ethical challenges. This is entirely appropriate. It resembles how, in the earlier life of the church, different groups and even religious orders developed their own, characteristic ethic—a way of living in community and participating in a shared set of goals. That experience needs to be expanded and applied to the entire church, so that what we are seeking is not uniformity but similarity.

Finally, in order to avoid being misunderstood, I believe that I must repeat my observation that the development of a meaningful, continuously scrutinized, and carefully elaborated, advisory form of normative ethics is essential for guiding persons who are attempting to navigate their way through making responsible behavioral choices for achieving the ends to which they want to commit their efforts. Norms do not have to be "absolute" to be important and have a bearing on how we make behavioral choices. When we realize their proper place, guiding us and not dictating to us, they become helpful and even friendly.

Conflicts of Interest: The author declares no conflict of interest.

References

Janssens, Louis. 1980. Artificial Insemination: Ethical Considerations. *Louvain Studies* 8: 3–29.
Knauer, Peter. 1965. La Détermination du bien et du mal moral par le principe du double effet. *Nouvelle Revue Théologique* 87: 356–76.
Knauer, Peter. 1967. The Hermeneutic Function of the Principle of Double Effect. *Natural Law Forum* 12: 132–62. [CrossRef]
Knauer, Peter. 1979. The Hermeneutic Function of the Principle of Double Effect. In *Moral Norms and Catholic Tradition*. Edited by Charles E. Curran and Richard A. McCormick. New York: Paulist Press, pp. 1–39.
Maslow, Abraham. 1987. *Motivation and Personality*. New York: Harper & Row, First published 1954.
Rokeach, Milton. 1973. *The Nature of Human Values*. New York: The Free Press.
Selling, Joseph A. 1998. The Human Person. In *Christian Ethics: An Introduction*. Edited by Bernard Hoose. London: Geoffrey Chapman, pp. 95–109.
Selling, Joseph A. 2016. *Reframing Catholic Theological Ethics*. Oxford: Oxford University Press.

© 2017 by the author. Licensee MDPI, Basel, Switzerland. This article is an open access article distributed under the terms and conditions of the Creative Commons Attribution (CC BY) license (http://creativecommons.org/licenses/by/4.0/).

Article

Reframing Catholic Ethics: Is the Person an Integral and Adequate Starting Point?

Lisa Sowle Cahill

Theology Department Faculty, Boston College, Chestnut Hill, MA 02467, USA; lisa.cahill@bc.edu

Received: 31 August 2017; Accepted: 23 September 2017; Published: 2 October 2017

Abstract: Joseph Selling rightly defines human intentions and motivations as part of human nature and an important determinant of the morality of personal actions. The thesis of this paper is that Selling's view of agency, as focused on the individual, must be expanded to include social relationships and the social constitution of selves and communities. This requires cross-cultural dialogue about human nature, the goods for persons and societies, and social ethics.

Keywords: Aquinas's ethics; Catholic theological ethics; Catholic moral theology; cross-cultural ethics; global ethics; HIV/AIDS; *Humanae vitae*; moral agency; personalism; practical reason

1. Introduction

Joseph Selling's *Reframing Catholic Theological Ethics*[1] is a brilliant recap and culmination of major streams of renewal in Catholic moral theology that flowed from the Second Vatican Council and that were, ironically, given impetus by the 1968 "birth control" encyclical *Humanae vitae*. Selling's key point is that the fullness of morality and moral agency cannot be captured by the simple evaluation of physical actions, guided by the "bottom line" of avoiding "intrinsically evil acts". Instead the intention and motivations of the agent are morally decisive, as he or she strives to realize important ends or goals in complex and changing situations. Context and intention are indispensable to an "integral and adequate" understanding of the person as a moral agent, to paraphrase the reference in *Gaudium et spes* to "the nature of the human person and his acts" (no. 51, and as elaborated in official commentary[2]).

My own engagement with this book will proceed in five steps.

1. I will set Selling's project in its post-Vatican II context. His work represents an important step forward in this context, especially because it expands moral analysis beyond individual actions to include the person's intentions.
2. I will consider the significance of our present, 21st century context, which is more consciously global, more differentiated, more intercultural, and more interreligious, than that of the four decades immediately following the Council. In this context, it is essential to give a fully relational and social interpretation of persons, and of the constitution of selfhood and agency.
3. I will propose that Selling's book sets up the progression to this new context very successfully, but follows through incompletely. I will focus specifically on the fifth and sixth of eight characteristics by which Selling defines the person "integrally and adequately considered", that is, the person as *both* fundamentally relational *and* a free and responsible self.

---

[1] Oxford: Oxford University Press, 2016.
[2] *Schema constitutionis pastoralis de ecclesia in mundo huius temporis: Expensio modorum partis secundae* (Vatican Press, 1965) 37–38; as cited in (McCormick 1982). *Gaudium et spes* itself does not explicitly use the frequently-invoked phrase "human person integrally and adequately considered". Instead, specifically addressing the harmonization of "conjugal love" and "the responsible transmission of life", it calls for "objective standards" based on "the nature of the human person and his acts" (no. 51).

4. I will add in two ways to Selling's discussion of Aquinas on intentionality and the natural law, with which I of course concur. First, I will take up further discussion of the goods or goals or ends at which intention aims. For "teleological" ethics, these are key. Then, I will introduce the topic of practical reason, the type of reason involved in moral knowledge and intention, and also the way in which we know our goods and ends.
5. I will illustrate the difference a more social, inductive, and global approach would make to the reframing of Catholic ethics, by mentioning one example introduced by Selling himself, that is, the problem of HIV/AIDS.[3]

2. The Vatican II Trajectory, of Which This Book Is a Part

A widened understanding of the scope of personal morality has been the keynote of post-Vatican II moral theology overall, both in its magisterial expressions and in its development by the "guild" of Catholic moral theologians. Since the establishment of the Council, Catholic moral theology has given a new priority to context, relationships, and relational goods and responsibilities, as well as to gospel values. For instance, even Paul VI and John Paul II try to situate the disordered character of contraception in the context of the love of a married couple, and the nature of family relationships. In 1980, Selling's teacher Louis Janssens[4] applied the lens of "the human person integrally and adequately considered" to the problem of artificial insemination, developing a general perspective found in a 1972 article of Karl Rahner, and refuting the pre-conciliar act-based analysis of Franz Hürth (Janssens 1980; Rahner 1972; Hürth 1946).[5] This more holistic, agent-centered trajectory follows upon the Enlightenment "turn to the subject". The subject's anti-dogmatic authority was modeled in different ways by Descartes, Locke, Kant, and Freud. Introduced to Council-era Catholic theology most notably by Karl Rahner, the turn to the subject has characterized Catholic theological ethics generally since the start of the Council.

In a seemingly contrary way, the notion of "intrinsically evil" or "intrinsically disordered" acts was clearly reiterated during the pontificate of John Paul II, especially in *Veritatis splendor* (no. 80). However, even when traditional norms about disordered acts were asserted, they were and are reinforced with reference to interpersonal and relational categories such as "the language of the body" and the "truth" of the marital bond. For example, according to John Paul II, the sexually articulated "language of the body"

> is the constitutive element of the communion of the persons. The persons—man and woman—become for each other a mutual gift. They become that gift in their masculinity and femininity, discovering the spousal significance of the body and referring it reciprocally to themselves in an irreversible manner—in a life-long dimension (Paul 1983).

Those who take issue with the way magisterial teaching after the Council continues to assert more or less the same norms in personalist guise share with their adversaries a more contextual view of moral realities and a more relational view of the agent. Typically, they also share a primary focus on the individual agent, illustrated for example by appeals to "conscience." Nevertheless, despite this turn to subjects and relationships, the 20th century debates in moral theology remained centered on the individual agent—his or her embodiment, relationships, intentions, and acts.

Selling's center of gravity is the contraception debate, as it was for traditionalist morality during the same time period. Page 3 of the book highlights "the extended controversy over contraception", and the last page (200) recommends that the idea of intrinsic evil be dropped from the vocabulary of "traditional, personal, and especially sexual morality". Sexual ethics and contraception come up

---

[3] I will not address the morality of means of preventing HIV transmission in themselves, nor whether they are effective. My focus will be on the view of the person that is implied by Selling's own discussion of this topic.
[4] See (Christie 1990).
[5] These are all discussed by McCormick in the essay cited in n. 1. See also (McCormick 1994).

multiple times elsewhere, for example on pages 17–19, 115, 171, 180, 186, and 196. The contraception debate as a whole has tended to focus on individual couples, and their conscientious yet "objective" decisions as personal agents.

Perhaps it is time that we all turn greater attention to the social and political aspects of sex and gender; to the intersection of gender, race, class, and economic inequality; and, in particular, to the difference perspectives from the global South might make to our methods and conclusions. For instance, one big difference in the way persons understand and exercise their agency derives from the tendency of some cultures to see the individual as the primary religious and moral point of reference, as contrasted to the tendency of more communal cultures in the global South to view the community as primal, and individual identity as constituted by relationship.

"I am because we are" is an African adage embedded in the African philosophy of *ubuntu* espoused by Nelson Mandela.[6] In this and similar worldviews, collective wellbeing and harmony among humans, nature, and the spiritual world are more important than individual choice and self-realization. (In more communal cultures, the person experiences the divine through spiritual beings and forces that interconnect communities, their members, and other creatures historically. In many African cosmologies, individual welfare is one with the community and subordinated to it[7]). In contrast, modern, capitalistic democracies in the global North tend to see the self as striving within social opportunities and constraints to maximize its own potential and happiness—of which relationships are a part, including a personal relationship to God.[8] Yet, if the person is socially constituted and socially accountable in a radical way, then moving from personal act to personal motivation, while important and necessary, still does not provide a big enough frame for a global theological ethics. I will return to this point when addressing Selling's characterization of the "multi-dimensionality" of the human person.

First, though, let us look more carefully at our 21st century context.

3. The 21st Century Context

In the present century, a more global consciousness increasingly pervades theological ethics. Under the influence of postmodern and postcolonial philosophies, our view of the person in community has expanded. In a basic though non-reductionist way, agents are *constituted by* the communities and relationships in which they are born and raised to be deliberating, deciding, and acting social subjects. Both persons and communities are accountable to the basic material and social needs of other persons and societies near and far. Paradoxically, complex networks and structures at once *dilute* personal responsibility for the (distant) other, and *magnify* that agency by enabling collective, structural action.

The writings of Pope Francis illustrate this shift of theological-ethical paradigm. Francis has decisively undermined the "objective physical act'" frame of moral judgment by asking divorced couples to discern their moral state within multiple relational obligations, by warning against a rush to judgment of homosexual persons, and by suggesting that contraception can be an appropriate response to the Zika virus. In *Laudato Si'*, he highlights collective responsibility for the natural environment and references structural protections, such as UN climate agreements. Although I believe that issues of war and violence, economic inequality, ecology, racism, and gender discrimination are more important than sexual ethics as such, it is obvious that all these issues are intertwined. I will today keep my focus on sexual ethics as most key to Selling's book, and due to constraints of time.

Much could be said about reframing Catholic ethics on the basis of *Laudato Si'*, but the more pertinent document here is *Amoris Laetitia*. The most widely discussed moral controversy behind this document is the ethical and religious significance of remarriage after divorce, represented by

---

[6] See (Onyebuchi Eze 2010).
[7] These are not only huge generalizations, but they would be much better approached by a thinker from the global South. See for example (Orobator 2008).
[8] See for example (Ortner 2006) and the appreciative yet provocative review by (Mukerji 2009).

ecclesial regulation of participation in the Eucharist. Going beyond this one issue, Francis proposed and embodied a new approach to Catholic theological ethics when he called two Synods on the Family to precede the eventual document, prepared for those by instituting processes of wide consultation; encouraged open discussion at the Synods themselves; provided a year between the two Synods, so that ideas could circulate and percolate in the Church at large; proposed in *Amoris Laetitia* an open and flexible ("ambiguous") resolution rather than a definitive policy; and referred the question of the Eucharist back to local dioceses and individual couples who, together with their pastors, are asked to consider their relational obligations holistically. We must regard the exclusion of women from the synodal consultations as a significant liability. Nevertheless, the message has been sent that moral discernment and agency are collective, inductive, and locally variable, even if responsible to larger, nonrelative goods.

Considering the diversity of standpoint that was in evidence during the Family Synods, we all have to acknowledge the limits of our perspectives, as Selling does when he identifies his own as that of "an older, white, male, Christian European inhabitant" (Selling 2016, p. 161). This is also true of Pope Francis! Still, the question here is not only about the starting point; it is about those to whom one is reaching out and those from whom one wishes to learn. Older, white men and women, Western Europeans or North Americans like myself, can benefit tremendously by engaging other standpoints. Through engagement, we can together realize the intercultural and interreligious potential of our future discipline of theological ethics.

4. Joseph Selling's Framework and Its Promising Trajectory

In Chapter 5, Selling defines "The Human Person Integrally and Adequately Considered" in eight points, of which I want to explore the interdependence of the fifth and the sixth (Selling 2016, pp. 137–46). These are: 5. "the human person stands in relation to other persons", and 6. "the human person becomes a conscious interiority, a subject". On the one hand, says Selling, our "intimate relationships" provide "the process of becoming human". Our culture, history, and relationships are all mediated through other persons. On the other hand, "the person is not simply a material, cultural, social, historical entity", but also "an inner self, a subject endowed with freedom and called to responsibility" (Selling 2016, pp. 142–43). This is beautifully said! Yet I wonder whether the dialectic of society and self also signifies that so single-minded a focus on "the person" as the governing category can no longer inspire an adequate frame for ethics. Should the title of this chapter be changed from "Morality and the Human Person" to "Moralities, Persons, and Communities"?

I titled this paper with a question: "Reframing Catholic Ethics: Is the Person an Integral and Adequate Starting Point?" My answer is that person is not an "integral" starting point because of the ongoing social constitution not only of the person, but also of moral knowledge, intention, and action. Similarly, the person is not an "'adequate" starting point because the communities and social relations that shape personal identity and agency are also essential. In addition to the person, we need to consider traditions and communities "integrally and adequately".

5. Aquinas on a Teleological Ethics and Practical Reason

An important contribution of Selling is to recover the thought of Thomas Aquinas in the service of his program, specifically on the importance of intention to the character of moral acts, and an interpretation of the natural law as not a series of specific laws, but the participation of the human creature in the eternal law or divine wisdom. With Aquinas, Selling believes that one's motivation is virtuous if one is attempting to accomplish a good (Selling 2016, pp. 62, 68). Selling thus relies on a teleological model of ethics for which, I would argue, ends or goods are actually more basic than intention.[9] This leads to two further issues: identifying the goods at which moral intention and action aim, and recognizing that we do so by means of practical reason.

Selling notes that both Aristotle and Aquinas were teleologists, for whom happiness is the ultimate goal or good, with Aquinas following Augustine in referring happiness (and virtue) to humanity's highest end and good, God. Selling underscores the biblical sources of this perspective in the ministry of Jesus and his preaching of the kingdom or reign of God.

While happiness as a comprehensive human end is widely recognized, the identification, interrelation, and priority of more limited temporal goods is a much more controversial territory. This is true whether one's approach is Christian or not. In my view, the identification and realization of common human goods in and through the reality of pluralism is one of the greatest challenges to Christian ethics today. Aquinas would say that we can avoid relativism by recognizing that some basic human goods are shared. Further, we can account for particularity by recognizing that moral reason is practical reason.

First, goods. Even if, as in the Christian view, moral agency and discernment are informed and guided by the theological virtues and the "infused" moral virtues, Christian ethics still relies heavily on natural knowledge of the natural inclinations of humans to goods that are shared across cultures, though instantiated differently. As salient instances, Aquinas offers the tendency of all things to stay in being, the tendency of all animals to mate and nurture their young, and the tendency of humans specifically to live cooperatively in political society, as well as to "seek to know the truth about God." Human beings share certain basic physical, psychospiritual, and social needs, such as for food, physical safety, human companionship, ritual connection to the transcendent, and political participation. However, the refinement of these goods in the concrete requires inductive experience, as well as cross-cultural elaboration and correction.

This brings us to practical reason. The inductive knowledge of basic goods and the contextual knowledge of specific goods are both functions of practical reason. (See Aquinas's treatment of the natural law in *Summa Theologiae*, I-II.Q94.a2). Practical reason is distinguished from speculative reason as reason about things to be done, and it deals with "contingent matters, about which human actions are concerned". In practical action, there is potential unclarity and diversity, "the more we descend to matters of detail" (a4). Pope Francis quotes Aquinas on exactly this point, when he calls for the specific discernment of cases in *Amoris Laetitia* (Chapter 8, no. 304). Selling does not discuss practical reason, but he does say that to make choices instigating action that leads to happiness, "one needs wisdom primarily practical wisdom (*phronesis*) which is oriented to practical choices".[10] Practical wisdom or prudence is the virtue of right practical reason.

6. The Example of HIV/AIDS

Consider an example introduced in Selling's first chapter: the use of condoms to prevent the transmission of HIV/AIDS in heterosexual marriage. I totally agree with Selling's conclusion that condoms should in such cases be an option. This is an example of practical reason, discerning in a specific kind of situation how to prioritize and realize competing goods, such as the marital bond, its sexual expression, children and new life, and the lives and health of the spouses. But what would we learn about the importance of these goods, their endangerment, and their order of priority, if we included experiences and theological-ethical analyses from the global South?[11] Globally, girls and women are hardest hit by new infections, including those who are married and are faithful to

---

[9] As Selling says, "a systematic method of ethical reflection and decision-making that takes goal-seeking as its point of departure is referred to as 'teleological'" (ibid., p. 26, cf. 103). He also speaks of "an intention as directed to a circumstantiated end", designating "a circumstantiated action as a behavior" (ibid., p. 170).
[10] (Ibid., p. 122).
[11] In fact, going back to 2004, the bishops of Africa have been the most vocal in supporting condom use for so-called "discordant couples", and in 2010, Pope Benedict opened the door to condom use to prevent disease transmission. See (Condoms4Life 2015).

their husbands. According to UNAIDS, adolescent girls and young women aged 15–24 years are at particularly high risk of HIV infection, accounting for 20% of new HIV infections among adults globally in 2015, despite accounting for just 11% of the adult population. In geographical areas with the higher HIV prevalence, the gender imbalance is more pronounced. In sub-Saharan Africa, adolescent girls and young women accounted for 25% of new HIV infections among adults, and women accounted for 56% of new HIV infections among adults. Harmful gender norms and inequalities, insufficient access to education and sexual and reproductive health services, poverty, food insecurity, and violence are at the root of the increased HIV risk of young women and adolescent girls (UNAIDS n.d.).

These women and girls become infected, not just because of some idea that condoms are intrinsically evil, but because of their unequal status in sexual relationships, married or unmarried, a status that is embedded in social structures generally, and maintained by both individual and collective agency. The women most vulnerable to AIDS typically lack the power to choose their spouse, refuse sex, demand that their husband wear a condom, or insist that he be faithful. In fact, condom use generally is rejected by African men for cultural reasons, not primarily because of Catholic teaching. When we look at the global picture of HIV/AIDS, we realize more deeply that the basic goods of life, human equality, moral freedom, social responsibility, marriage, sex, and family are all profoundly implicated, in culturally varied ways, that go far beyond condom use.

Stigma and discrimination exacerbate lack of treatment and the spread of the disease in the global South. "In approximately half of countries with available data between 2009 and 2014, over 50% of women and men aged 15–49 years reported they would not buy vegetables from a shopkeeper living with HIV" (UNAIDS n.d.). If a married man learns he is infected, the blame will be cast upon his wife, and she will be repudiated and ostracized in many cases, as a danger and a disgrace to the community as a whole. If a woman has HIV/AIDS, she will hide her condition due to these same consequences. This signals a high likelihood that neither spouse would share their disease status or initiate condom use. While affected Catholic couples who are honest about their situation should certainly be advised to use condoms, gender inequality, stigma, and poverty are much greater obstacles to morally responsible sex than Catholic Church teaching about condoms.

Further, we should ask whether Catholic models of gender complementarity are a contributing factor, in addition to whether our insistence on framing questions of sexual ethics as they are seen in the U.S. and Western Europe prevents us from confronting the much direr sexual injustices that the less privileged suffer. We in the global North can learn from worldwide realities. We must also recognize our own complicity in creating social conditions that help create poverty and injustice.

The relevance of Catholic theological ethics to HIV/AIDS cannot be "reframed" without the insights of cultures and theologies in Africa, Asia, and Latin America, nor without explicit consideration of gender, race, economic status, and sexual orientation. Three book titles dealing with AIDS, Catholic theology, and ethics give a quick indication of the analytical scope now required to frame the theological ethics of AIDS: *When God's People Have HIV/AIDS: An Approach to Ethics*; *Calling for Justice Throughout the World: Catholic Women Theologians on the HIV/AIDS Pandemic*; and *HIV and AIDS in Africa: Christian Reflection, Public Health, Social Transformation* (Cimperman 2005; Jo Iozzio et al. 2009; Azetsop 2016).

Selling's book skillfully and admirably expands our vision of what an agent is and does. Yet it remains centered on the individual agent as envisioned at the time of Vatican II. Nevertheless, Selling decisively opens the door to the further steps needed if Catholic theological ethics is to be transformed for a new century by the contributions of plural cultures and religions. Most basically, he contextualizes the agent's behavior, and therefore also the intentional and motivated agent him- or herself. He states explicitly that virtues are cultural and historical, that they are shaped by cultural traditions, and that they must "respond to specific, challenging situations" (Selling 2016, p. 158). This move, taken seriously, leads us ineluctably to a reframing of Catholic ethics that is cross-communal and dialogic, because together our cultural traditions lead us to a deeper appreciation of what we share as human beings, and an appreciation of our vital differences.

Conflicts of Interest: The author declares no conflict of interest.

References

Azetsop, Jacquineau, ed. 2016. *HIV and AIDS in Africa: Christian Reflection, Public Health, Social Transformation*. Maryknoll: Orbis.

Christie, Dolores L. 1990. *Adequately Considered: An American Perspective on Louis Janssens' Personalist Morals*. Louvain: Peeters, p. 3.

Cimperman, Maria. 2005. *When God's People Have HIV/AIDS: An Approach to Ethics*. Maryknoll: Orbis.

Condoms4Life. 2015. *The Catholic Bishops and Condoms: Statements and Actions Supporting Condom Use to Prevent the Spread of HIV*. Washington: Catholics for Choice, Available online: http://www.catholicsforchoice.org/issues_publications/the-catholic-bishops-and-condoms-statements-and-actions-supporting-condom-use-as-part-of-an-hiv-prevention-strategy/ (accessed on 12 January 2016).

Hürth, Franz. 1946. La fécondation artificielle: Sa valeur morale et juridique. *Nouvelle Revue Théologique* 68: 413.

Janssens, Louis. 1980. Artificial Insemination: Ethical Considerations. *Louvain Studies* 8: 3–29.

Jo Iozzio, Mary, Elsie Miranda, and Mary Roche Doyle, eds. 2009. *Calling for Justice throughout the World: Catholic Women Theologians on the HIV/AIDS Pandemic*. London: Bloomsbury Academic.

McCormick, Richard A. 1982. Notes on Moral Theology: 1981. *Theological Studies* 43: 69. [CrossRef]

McCormick, Richard A. 1994. *Corrective Vision: Explorations in Moral Theology*. Lanham: Rowman and Littlefield, pp. 201–2.

Mukerji, Chandra. 2009. Book Review: Anthropology and Social Theory: Culture, Power, and the Acting Subject. *American Journal of Sociology* 115: 560–63. [CrossRef]

Onyebuchi Eze, Michael. 2010. *Intellectual History of Contemporary South Africa*. London: Palgrave Macmillan, pp. 190–91.

Orobator, Agbonkhianmeghe E. 2008. *Theology Brewed in an African Pot*. Maryknoll: Orbis.

Ortner, Sherry. 2006. *Anthropology and Social Theory: Culture, Power, and the Acting Subject*. Durham: Duke University Press.

Paul, John, II. 1983. General Audience of 5 January 1983. Available online: http://www.ewtn.com/library/PAPALDOC/jp2tb103.htm (accessed on 10 January 2016).

Rahner, Karl. 1972. The Problem of Genetic Manipulation. In *Theological Investigations*. New York: Herder and Herder, vol. 9, pp. 225–52.

Selling, Joseph A. 2016. *Reframing Catholic Theological Ethics*. Oxford: Oxford University Press.

UNAIDS. n.d. Global AIDS Update 201. Available online: http://www.unaids.org/sites/default/files/media_asset/global-AIDS-update-2016_en.pdf (accessed on 12 January 2017).

© 2017 by the author. Licensee MDPI, Basel, Switzerland. This article is an open access article distributed under the terms and conditions of the Creative Commons Attribution (CC BY) license (http://creativecommons.org/licenses/by/4.0/).

Article

Goal-Oriented Ethics: Framing the Goal-Setting Concretely

Mathew Illathuparampil

Department of Christian Ethics, St. Joseph Pontifical Seminary, Aluva 683102, India; illathuparampilmathew@gmail.com

Received: 17 August 2017; Accepted: 7 October 2017; Published: 17 October 2017

Abstract: Joseph Selling, professor emeritus from KU Leuven, Belgium, recently made a significant contribution towards ethical methodology. It is in fact a continuation of the in-house conversations that have been in vogue about methods in moral reasoning since Vatican II in the discipline called theological ethics. What is specific about Selling's attempt is that he re-orients or reframes the evaluation of the moral event to consider human intentionality or motivation before considering human behavior or human acts. He convincingly establishes his method by a meticulous reading of Thomas Aquinas. This paper is a response to the goal-oriented ethics that he has posited. As illustrated below, this paper evaluates the goal-oriented approach as solid and sufficient. While fully endorsing this approach, this paper argues that the process of ethical goal-setting is to be framed concretely. In a concrete historical context, so that a goal-oriented approach fully serves its purpose, this paper proposes that it is to be reinforced by four supportive pillars, which are in fact assumed by Selling in his work. They are openness to human sciences, conversation among various narratives, positing a theological frame for ethical reasoning, and recourse to non-discursive reasoning.

Keywords: ethical methodology; Joseph Selling; goal-oriented approach; non-discursive reasoning; narratives

1. Introduction

Book-length discussions on ethical methodology are rather rare. Rarer still are proposals for reframing theological ethics. Joseph Selling, with his book *Reframing Catholic Theological Ethics*, (Selling 2016) has nevertheless travelled into that less trodden terrain. While it is a matter of great accomplishment for him, for the company of Christian ethicists, it poses a great task—to grasp, evaluate, and integrate the major claims that he makes in this work into contemporary ethical reasoning, particularly ethical methodology.

Selling reframes Catholic theological ethics by positing a goal-oriented approach to ethical thinking in the place of the traditionally held act-oriented approach. In the act-oriented approach, what a person does figures more prominently in the total moral event than what a person is or what she or he should become. He comes to this understanding by a meticulous reading of Thomas Aquinas. Thus, he is able to affirm: "If I had to single out one thing that characterizes Thomas' uniqueness in our Western, ethical tradition, it would have to be his insistence that the moral evaluation of human activity begins with the integrity of moral intention, which is subsequently followed by a consideration of behavioral options. Who one is, the moral character that the acing person exhibits, is by far more important than the sometimes clumsy, uninformed, or simply mistaken behavioral choices that we make" (Selling 2016, p. 82).

The end or circumstantiated intention becomes very crucial in the goal-oriented pattern of reasoning. As well argued in his work, the goals of ethical living are set over against three overarching points of reference. First, in traditional terms, virtues; second, according to Vatican II, in terms of human dignity; third, following the lead of Vatican II and as expounded by some ethicists, in terms of the paradigm of the human person adequately and integrally considered (Christie 1990; Janssens 1980).

What Selling graphically presents in the book could be summarily understood as a conceptual scheme in the sense of a systemic way or model for thinking about methodological issues in ethics. It is a way of organizing moral experience in a coherent way. It makes use of the traditional categories that give form to what he meaningfully calls a moral event (Selling 2016, p. 62). As an abstract working conceptual scheme, this is certainly closer to reality than the traditional act-centred model, historically, precast to help the confessors.

When someone wants to take his/her intention towards the goal of ethical living in regard to any of the three points of reference/standards, content-wise it ceases to be simple. For in itself, the process of ethical goal setting stomachs a sort of historical conditioning. This means that the overarching justifications/legitimations of ethical goal setting do not enjoy universalizability or wider communicability. First, let us consider the case of virtues. One can choose to realize cardinal virtues, or any other virtue, which we can imagine. But every (category of) virtue represents a historical, political, or even ideological life-world. To some degree, at least in certain cases, virtues reveal a sort of theological determination as well. For example, in spite of their historical affinity, the same virtues in the Greek city states and the Christian West did not have the exact same meanings. St. Ambrose and St. Augustine Christianized Greek virtues vary in their interpretation. Similarly, what is virtuous in medieval feudal society, for instance, freedom, would not be so in a modern democratic society.

Second, we consider human dignity. In spite of its wide political assertion through the concept of human rights, human dignity is subject to differing interpretation. For example, when Albert the Great defined a person as "a subject distinguished by dignity" he was in a way defining human identity in terms of human dignity. But Thomas does not go so far. He, for example, held that human beings could lose their dignity if they deviate from the rational order by sinning, and that it is not necessarily bad to kill such sinners, despite the fact that to kill an innocent person in possession of natural dignity is evil. Be it also remarked that Aquinas uses the phrase *dignitas humana* very rarely—in the *Summa Theologiae* only once (II-II 64,2). Perceptions of human dignity are in reality conditioned by different features of human reality: human nature; God-relatedness; the faculty of reason; or recognition within society. Depending on the interpretation of human dignity on account of the above parameters, one may choose different ethical approaches to female genital mutilation, experimentation with human subjects, punishments, human cloning, stem cell research, etc.

Third, let us turn quickly to the paradigm of the human person adequately and integrally considered. It gives due attention to the historicity of the human person. Nonetheless, the paradigm of the human person adequately and integrally considered may not be able to interpret or account for certain human goals and the concomitant intention and the subsequent behavior within that paradigm. For example, think about an ethical goal that involves a break from the integrity of the parameters of the human person adequately and integrally considered. Take, for instance, one's choice of martyrdom or ascetic life. Such instances are so radical that, for the sake of a particularly highly esteemed goal, one chooses to relinquish the essential parameters of the human person adequately and integrally considered. To illustrate this point further, when someone opts for martyrdom for the sake of a religious goal, s/he is willing to surrender some of the parameters of the human person adequately and integrally considered, such as her/his corporeality, her/his being part of the material world, and her/his historicity. In this situation, the ethical goal or intention of the one who opted for martyrdom escapes the evaluative parameters of the human person adequately and integrally considered.

2. Four Supportive Pillars

Briefly, what I am trying to argue here is this: as an abstract methodological scheme, the legitimation for making a goal-oriented approach is solid and sufficient. While fully endorsing this approach, I believe that the process of ethical goal-setting is to be framed concretely. For goal setting does not float above historical and contingent realities from which we simply deduce values and norms. But in a concrete historical context, so that a goal-oriented approach serves its purpose, I propose that it is to be reinforced by four supportive pillars. They are mentioned in the book of Selling in various places. For example, when he describes "the virtuous person" he is circumspect enough to state that one is a very situated person (Selling 2016, p. 161). The kinds of virtue enlisted by him do not make any claim universal; rather, they are historically conditioned by elements such as geography, culture, and religion. But in this attempt, I shall capture, expand, and bring them into focus. This is one way in which we can ensure that ethical goal-setting is practically well-founded, drawing on human experience or a wider grasp of what it means to be human. We now turn to a thumbnail sketch of those four pillars.

2.1. Openness to Human Sciences

It is quite understandable that ethical reflections or conclusions are considerably informed by existing scientific knowledge about the human person and the world. Aristotelian or Thomistic ethics is not an exception to this rule. In the medieval period, ethics was backed more by philosophy and theology than by human sciences. Openness to human sciences such as biology, anthropology, psychology, sociology, and medicine will surely shed light on what it means to be human. Even the claims of equal human dignity for all men and women would not be possible without the support of science. Think about the past example: women were ill-treated considering them as "defective males," a tradition attributed to Aristotle, because of the ancient underdeveloped biology. On account of the then prevalent "scientific data" that woman "requires a smaller quantity of nutriment," it was customary in his society to allow girls and women to eat only half as much as boys and men (Aristotle 1965, 608b.14).

Openness to science has yet to become a parameter to determine our ethical goals. A good example would be the attempt to distinguish between homosexual acts and homosexual orientation. Openness to science has still to enlighten various aspects of ethical discourse in distinguishing between homosexual acts and homosexual orientation. Science can ascertain whether sexual orientation ranges along a continuum, from exclusive attraction to the opposite sex to exclusive attraction to the same sex, or whether homosexual acts can be explained scientifically in any other way. If ethical discussions do not depend on scientific data, they could be led by identity labels given to sexual behaviors by different cultures. A scientific indication of the moment of brain death becomes significant in regard to justifying organ harvesting from a cadaver. While admitting the role of science in making sound ethical discourse, we need to underline that science does not, nay cannot, adequately make value statements. Granted, there are still debatable claims made by "science," which have apparent ramifications for ethics. For example, the discussions regarding "criminal genes." Similarly, a "scientific" approach to selecting the beneficiaries of charity may not always satisfy certain ethical aspects. In spite of these reservations, openness to advancements in science is vital for keeping ethical goals in the right perspective. We may not need refer to science on a daily basis in setting our ethical goals. We presume it more often than not. But those who make ethical teachings need it very much.

2.2. Conversation among Narratives

Selling establishes convincingly and reiterates that, in a moral event, the first question is what one wants to accomplish. More precisely, it refers to the ethical goals. He acknowledges that each of us may choose different ways to accomplish what we may identify as virtues. In that process, he argues, persons are to be helped to construct a narrative that highlights virtuous living (Selling 2016, p. 197). Going a step further, let me propose that, to enrich the process of goal setting, we need a healthy interface of different narratives. Think about two prominent and closely related figures of the New Testament: John the Baptist and Jesus. Both had different behavioral patterns because both had different goals set—because both of them operated from two different narratives. The Baptist was following the prophetic narrative of the Old Testament, while Jesus was following and creating a narrative of the kingdom of God. One can say broadly that John the Baptist belonged to the prophetic narratives, which usually consist of warnings, condemnations, exhortations, advice, and eventually encouragement. They also often tended to announce curses. They insisted vehemently on the justice of God. But Jesus introduced a fairly different narrative of the kingdom of God where the mercy of God prevailed. Their narratives were so different that at one point John the Baptist was scandalized at the behavior of Jesus, and asked him, are you the promised one? (Mt 11:3).

Goal setting has to attend to the underlying narrative that persons carry about their different values, ideals, and virtues. For example, according to the narrative that one follows, one may oppose violence or engage in violence. Parenting, respect to life, respect to differences, conflict resolution, and a host of other vital concerns are driven by a certain kind of a narrative that persons follow, and accordingly they will have different ethical goals set for themselves.

In a multi-religious and pluri-cultural context, there must be occasions for one narrative to converse with, if not confront, another narrative. This has many implications, especially when ethics is done in the public square. In a country like India, for instance, when the Catholic Church argues against abortion in public, for many people it is simply unintelligible. For different parties in this conversation follow different narratives. For similar reasons, the work of Mother Theresa, in taking care of dying and sure-to-die persons, was not equally appreciated across the globe. Close exchange between the diverse narratives of people is mandatory to keep the ethical goals of people purified and intelligible to others.

What every culture does ultimately is the organization of human consciousness on a collective level. "What is religion if it is not a powerful agency for the organization of consciousness?" (Hefner 2003, p. 188). The values we hold, the moral judgements that we make, and the decisions that we take depend to a great extent on how our consciousness is organized (Hefner 2003, p. 187). Religion seeks to organize consciousness according to the deepest realities of life, the realities that relativize all others. It suggests that our perceptions of right/wrong and good/bad depend heavily on how our consciousness is organized by religious narratives.

Morality depends very much on how the community and narratives shape an individual. The rootedness of a person in a community of life and meaning inserts her/him into a narrative. Conversation among different narratives may ultimately require reference to a "grand narrative" (if we can use that expression and withstanding the critique of postmodernism) effective for goal-setting. Perhaps the best candidate for such a grand narrative would be the Kingdom of God, which again immediately falls into small narratives in practice. This leads us to the next step.

2.3. Theological Frame for Ethical Goal Setting

The ethical scheme proposed by Selling rightly focuses on what one wants to accomplish—the goals. From a goal follows the attitude and action within a given circumstance to realize that ethical goal. But choosing (or not choosing) a goal is closely related to the question of why one should choose that particular goal, which is likely to be demanding. That demanding part is usually expressed through commandments or norms.

In real situations, ethical goals are set within larger life goals. It could be something similar to this scenario: a person has many options of games, such as basketball, cricket, and football. Once s/he opts for a particular game, s/he is bound to follow its rules. But the important question is why does s/he choose that game? In a much similar way, a question would surface: why should one place him-/herself in the parameters of particular goals to become ethical? The answer to this question will go beyond the boundaries of ethics.

The traditional answer to this question is as straightforward as to go to heaven. The larger life goal that justifies an ethical goal is indicated in the question of the Pharisee, what good deed must I do to inherit eternal life? (Mt 19:16). Jesus in his turn makes a shift, saying "if you want to be perfect," follow the commandments. Jesus later embellishes it in relation to entering the Kingdom of God.

This exchange of question and answer bears theological content. That reveals the scope of theological ethics, which brings out the motivational aspect of ethical goal setting. Ethics permeated by theology shall ineluctably result in better communicability in a faith community.

Vatican II in its document Optatam totius no. 16 wanted theological disciplines to make use of the Bible: "The students are to be formed with particular care in the study of the Bible, which ought to be, as it were, the soul of all theology. After a suitable introduction they are to be initiated carefully into the method of exegesis ... " Until the period of the Council, scriptures were used in ethics only in a proof-texting manner. After establishing their conclusions with the support of natural law and philosophy, ethicists used to refer to scriptural passages as an additional proof for their conclusions. They did so using the Bible quite literally. After the Council, there were many attempts to integrate scripture or theology into ethical reflections. It is interesting to note that more than forty years after Vatican II, the Vatican's Pontifical Biblical Commission issued a document in 2008 entitled: Bible and Morality: Biblical Roots of Christian Conduct. However, the integration of scripture into ethical reasoning is still due, which is also in view of a goal-oriented approach to ethics.

2.4. Non-Discursive Reasoning

A goal-oriented approach to ethics rightly recognizes the proportion between the goal and the means chosen and the inevitable scope of the evil tolerated. Circumstantiated intention presupposes a sort of calculation of the good achieved and the evil avoided or tolerated. Sometimes it can be a vague kind of calculation, for it need not always enjoy any sort of scientific or mathematical precision. It could better be called a perceptive evaluation of the good achieved and the evil avoided or tolerated. In the process of setting ethical goals, there is a rational calculation of the circumstance and material facts. For example, environmental protection has become part of our ethical goals thanks to the recent calculated prediction of the impact of environmental degradation on human life and the ecosystem. In determining the core demand of justice (what one owes to another), there is some sort of a rational evaluation of the claims to and fro. When a business corporation chooses to do its social responsibility by spending part of its profit, it involves a good amount of calculative reasoning. Briefly, ethical goal setting is usually supposed to be rational and calculative. In the scheme presented by Selling, this discursively rational overtone is clear. His conversation partners, including Thomas, followed this line. This is an indubitable part of goal setting.

In the process of setting goals, along with the discursive part, there is a complex structure of affections and judgements that are part of the goal that we set. Consciously or not, an *affective affirmation* (Farley 2011, p. 144) of what is set as the goal takes place. We do not just know the goal, but we experience being morally obliged. But we do not know exactly how we come to that experience of being morally obliged. A few attempts have been made to refer to that level of knowing: St. Augustine in his *Confessions* (9.9) said, "my love is my weight." Thomas seems to assume that principles of natural moral law break through into human consciousness (*Summa Theologia* II-II, 90, a.1 ad 1, q.91, a.2). In philosophy, David Hume spoke of "moral sentiments" as an inbuilt affective trigger (Hume 1968, III.2.5).

Ethical purposiveness, I believe, must also allow credence for the non-discursive epistemological elements, for humans are not only coming to know moral truths, but are also capturing them through non-discursive faculties. These would include a sense of fairness, moral imagination, discernment, intuitions, aesthetic perceptions of what is right and wrong, and a sense of the sublime, all of which escape deductive rational calculations. There are ethical goals chosen by people that in no way are explained by a simple discursive rationality. That means, in ethical goal setting, men and women are also guided by extra-discursive reasoning.

A moral approach, if it is to be relevant and applicable to situations and intentions of real human beings, cannot simply be governed by discursive reason alone, for human rationality is also comprised of non-discursive elements (Illathuparampil 2009, p. 150). Reason always seeks or establishes something to justify itself from outside. But human beings may set ethical goals even without reference to a justification from outside (rational ground). Rationality seeks to establish meaning or justification by a sort of "coherence of intersubjective relationships" (Gaziaux 2011, p. 132). There is no such thing as a discursive justification in poetry (*poiesis*). That is why Socrates said in Plato's *Republic* (607b), "there is from old a quarrel between philosophy and poetry." However, we do not condemn poetry as stupidity. It is no surprise that an ethical system that heavily drew from abstract philosophy became incapable of addressing non-discursive ways of knowing or judgements. In philosophical ethics, Kant represents the epitome of this approach. He sought to guarantee the autonomy of morality by grounding morality neither in religious or metaphysical beliefs, nor in any empirical account of humanity, but in rationality *qua* rationality. Thus, the feelings and the history of the agent are not at all taken into consideration. It assumes and even celebrates objectivity in moral life attained by freeing moral judgements from the subjective story of the agent.

When a goal-oriented moral approach is open to non-discursive style of reasoning, it would be able to accommodate apparently erratic moral elements in our ethical reasoning. For example, Adam Smith in his *Theory of Moral Sentiments* argued that, however selfish a person can be, there are principles in his nature that interest him in the fortune of others. One of these "principles" is sympathy ((Smith 1976, I.(I) 1.1)). Only a sort of moral imagination will allow you to hold that the most selfish person can also be sympathetic to others. No axiomatic-deductive system will be able to perceive this complex human trait.

3. Conclusions

Sustained discussions on ethical methodology require a great amount of familiarity with technical terms and the history of the development of theological ethics. Reframing of Catholic theological ethics proposed by Selling demands the same from the readers as well his conversation partners. Therefore, easy access to arguments of this work might be limited to experts in the field. But the scope of its implications certainly extends to pastoral practice, church life, and moral reasoning in general. What this paper has not done is refute any claims of this work; rather, one aspect of it has been embellished, namely, a goal-oriented ethical approach, so as to make it more perceptible and practicable in concrete.

This paper proposes that a goal-oriented moral approach is to be reinforced by four methodological pillars such as openness to human sciences, conversation among narratives, a theological frame for ethical goal setting, and non-discursive reasoning. Naturally, this raises the question of what superstructure these four pillars can together keep in focus as one sets his/her own ethical goals. This process cannot be served by any blind technique or an overarching framework, but it would demand the goal-setting person to sensitize him-/herself to these vital areas. It depends very much on the moral sensitivity of the goal-setting person. The goal-setting person is thus required to integrate the informational, affective, and motivational elements contained in moral reasoning and implied by the four pillars. As one becomes perceptive to these four methodological pillars, overcoming possible cognitive biases and affective blinders, his/her goal-oriented moral approach becomes less fallible.

Conflicts of Interest: The author declares no conflict of interest.

References

Aristotle. 1965. *History of Animals*. Translated by A. L. Peck. Harvard: Harvard University Press.

Christie, Dolores L. 1990. *Adequately Considered: An American Perspective on Louis Janssens' Personalist Morals*. Louvain Theological & Pastoral Monographs, 4. Leven: Peters.

Farley, Margaret A. 2011. A Framework for Moral Discernment. In *Catholic Theological Ethics Past, Present, and Future: The Trento Conference*. Edited by James F. Keenan. Bangalore: TPI.

Gaziaux, Éric. 2011. In What Sense is Moral Theology Rational? In *Catholic Theological Ethics Past, Present, and Future: The Trento Conference*. Edited by James F. Keenan. Bangalore: TPI.

Hefner, Philip. 2003. Religion in the Context of Culture, Theology and Global Ethics. *Zygon* 38: 185–95. [CrossRef]

Hume, David. 1968. *Treatise of Human Nature*. Edited by Lewis Amherst Selby-Bigge. Oxford: Clarendon, III.2.5.
Illathuparampil, Mathew. 2009. *Technology and Ethical Ambiguity*. New Delhi: Global Vision Publishing House.
Janssens, Louis. 1980. Artificial Insemination: Ethical Considerations. *Louvain Studies* 8: 3–29.
Selling, Joseph A. 2016. *Reframing Catholic Theological Ethics*. Oxford: Oxford University Press.
Smith, Adam. 1976. *The Theory of Moral Sentiments*. Edited by A. L. Macfie and D. D. Raphael. Oxford: Oxford University Press.

 © 2017 by the author. Licensee MDPI, Basel, Switzerland. This article is an open access article distributed under the terms and conditions of the Creative Commons Attribution (CC BY) license (http://creativecommons.org/licenses/by/4.0/).

Article

Pope Francis and Joseph Selling: A New Approach to Mercy in Catholic Sexual Ethics

Mary Catherine O'Reilly-Gindhart

Theology and Religious Studies, University of Glasgow, Glasgow, Scotland, G12 8QQ, UK; m.oreilly-gindhart.1@research.gla.ac.uk

Received: 17 August 2017; Accepted: 8 November 2017; Published: 3 December 2017

Abstract: Since the Apostolic Exhortation of *Amoris Laetitia* in May 2016 and Apostolic Letter *Misericordia et Misera* in November 2016, Pope Francis has stirred a new discussion on mercy and the role of mercy in certain matters of sexual ethics including divorced, remarried, and cohabiting couples. During the same year, moral theologian Joseph A. Selling published a revolutionary book which provides a new vision of virtues and examines how people consider and arrive at ethical judgements. This article examines Pope Francis's understanding of mercy using Selling's method of the "virtuous trapezium" as a way to actively illustrate Pope Francis's new approach to matters concerning Catholic sexuality. In matters of human sexuality, the Catholic moral tradition has focused for years on an act-centered morality, but Selling's method instead considers the goals of ethical living before making an ethical judgment. This article contributes to the current discussion in theological ethics concerning Pope Francis's recent pronouncements on mercy and Catholic sexual ethics, as well as brings into conversation Selling's new method and approach to understanding virtue.

Keywords: mercy; Catholic; sexual ethics; *Amoris Laetitia*; *Misericordia et Misera*; cohabitation; divorced; remarried; Joseph Selling

1. Introduction

Joseph Selling's *Reframing Catholic Theological Ethics* has changed how Catholics can understand and exercise virtues and it has prompted a discussion on how to further perceive Pope Francis's new approach of mercy in certain matters of sexual ethics. The virtue of mercy has become a prominent message of Pope Francis's papacy since 2013. Pope Francis has set a new pastoral tone within the Catholic Church through his promotion of mercy in pastoral situations relating to sexual matters, including divorced and remarried Catholics and cohabiting Catholic couples. In this article, I examine how Catholics can use Joseph Selling's method of the "virtuous trapezium" as a way to understand the virtue of mercy, and how to implement mercy in their daily lives. Mercy is a virtue, and like all virtues, mercy cannot be practiced in the same way in every situation by all Catholics at any given time. The "virtuous trapezium" is a method which allows Catholics to evaluate and engage in the virtues. This article focuses on how Catholics can live out and exercise Pope Francis's message of mercy in matters of sexual ethics by using Selling's method the "virtuous trapezium". Overall, Joseph Selling and Pope Francis are very similar in their approaches to help the Church become less concerned with an act-centered morality and more concerned with the situations and the reality that everyday Catholics find themselves living in. Selling's "virtuous trapezium" allows Catholics to individually and effectively exercise the virtue of mercy concerning matters of sexual ethics in a new way which endorses Pope Francis's message of focusing on individual situations rather than ideal situations. This article is separated into four parts. Firstly, I examine Joseph Selling's definition of what a virtue is and how his vision of the virtues should be understood in Catholicism today. I do not go into detail about all aspects of his approach, but focus on articulating what Selling calls the "virtuous trapezium" and show how his approach opens up "a space for a much broader understanding of the meaning of ethical living" (Selling 2016, p. 160 Secondly, I reflect on the pronouncements of mercifulness made by Pope Francis in *Amoris Laetitia* and his Apostolic Letter *Misericordia et Misera*, including the Pope's direct connection between mercy and certain matters that concern Catholic teaching on sexuality. A question that I attempt to answer is: how should Catholics apply what Pope Francis has said about mercy to matters of sexual ethics? Last, I discuss how Catholics can use Selling's approach and method of the "virtuous trapezium" as a tool to implement mercy in their daily lives, giving special attention to the merciful tone Pope Francis has set for certain "irregular situations" concerning topics within sexual ethics. I will also give a real-life example of how Pope Francis's new pastoral approach of mercy can be seen and understood using Selling's new approach to virtue. In this article I hope to demonstrate that Joseph Selling's new method offers a tangible approach and tool to engage Catholics in "irregular situations" across the world.

2. Joseph Selling's New Approach to Virtue

Joseph Selling's *Reframing Catholic Theological Ethics* has changed how Catholics can understand and apply virtues to their everyday life situations. My discussion is focused on the sixth chapter of Selling's book, "Seeking the End: A Fresh Look at the Concept of Virtue", which helps Catholics consider and arrive at ethical judgments (Selling 2016, p. 9). This chapter identifies and explains virtue in a new way. Virtues are no longer to be thought of as an ideal on a pedestal, but rather a version that reflects the realities of everyday lived experience. Selling's method, entitled the "virtuous trapezium" is similar to theologian Peter Knauer's concept of the "square" of judging virtues (ibid., p. 154). Selling's approach is thought out in the geometrical shape of a trapezium. In the upper right and left corners of the trapezium there are two complementary virtues. On the bottom of the virtuous trapezium, in the right and left hand corners, are two extremes that correlate with the above complementary virtues. In the center of the trapezium is a real-life situation in which one might find oneself and which demands ethical consideration and reasoning. The trapezium figure consists of different elements, which are correlated to each other in a certain way. The complementary virtues in the upper corners of the trapezium are on a continuum, and the two extremes of these virtues are below and directly parallel to them. The paradigm is not a fixed or concrete structure that is absolute and unchanging, since it changes depending on every person's unique situation. This allows Catholics in different cultural, social, economic, or political situations to effectively use this one model as a way to understand and apply virtue in their daily lives. Selling is adamant that "the focal point of moral living is not the virtues themselves, but the identification of the human situations that the virtues are attempting to address." (ibid., p. 156). He believes that virtues are helpful in identifying the essence of moral living; however, it "is not the virtues themselves that denote the ends or goals to be sought after" (ibid., p. 157). Selling's method does not advocate for a person to pursue abstract views of virtues. His idea consists of finding a mode of relating to others in a concrete circumstance where a whole cluster of virtues are at play and need discernment and reflection. This is different from the traditional Catholic understanding, which presents virtues as ideals to live up to. Selling's notion assesses virtues as they pertain to our individual situations. There is no simple "recipe" according to Selling. He says that "attempting to create such a recipe would lead to endless accounting of detail [for example], if the situation includes factors A, B, C, D, and K, an appropriate goal towards which to strive might be X; but if the factors include A, B, C, D, and M, then perhaps a very different response is called for." (ibid., p. 155). Selling suggests complementary virtues are the key to moral living. What Selling means by complementary virtues is taken from Peter Knauer, who suggests that every virtue has a complement (ibid., p. 155). For example, the virtue bravery and the virtue caution are complementary virtues to each other. Complementary virtues "identify areas of human living, situations that persons may (or may not) face in the course of their lives."(ibid., p. 157). This is why Selling's virtuous trapezium works and is a great approach for Catholics because his method is not choosing between two extremes, but instead involves a "continuum between two virtues, each of which represents a 'qualified' (moderated) version of an extreme." (ibid., p. 156). (See Figure 1.) For Selling, complementary virtues are "on a continuum, and the nature of one's intention, one's commitment to realize an end, occurs somewhere between the two." (ibid., pp. 154–55). Foolhardiness and cowardice are the extremes of the complementary virtues of bravery and caution. In the middle of the trapezium is a situation that someone might find themselves in. The situation that is presented here is "dealing with dangerous situations or with opposition". Selling's approach to understanding virtue uses real life human situations to call into discussion complementary virtues as well as their extremes. The virtuous person will identify an appropriate response, which falls within the bandwidth of prudent approaches to the situation. This will avoid the two extremes and fall somewhere within the spectrum of virtuous behaviours. This trapezium approach helps explain "why it is unrealistic to judge all behaviours by the same, exact expectations." (ibid., p. 157). Selling's method offers a "thicker understanding of the goals of ethical living." (ibid., p. 12). I believe this method can be used by Catholics to live out Pope Francis's approach of mercy in certain "irregular situations" that concern human sexuality. Instead of putting virtues on a pedestal, which traditional Catholic teaching has done, Selling argues for virtues to be experienced and understood in discernment of individual situations by looking at a virtue's complement rather than idolizing and living up to one specific virtue. Selling's method of the "virtuous trapezium" is a good tool for individual Catholics to use in the distinct context of their personal lives, and can be used by Catholics across the world and in a myriad of different situations.

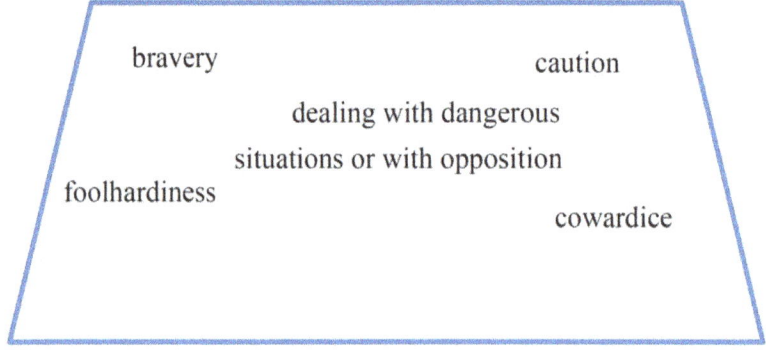

Figure 1. Bravery and Caution Virtuous Trapezium (See Selling 2016, p. 234).

3. Mercy in *Amoris Laetitia* and *Misericordia et Misera*

In *Amoris Laetitia* and *Misericordia et Misera*, Pope Francis has called for pastoral change concerning the virtue of mercy in certain sexual matters. These sexual matters concern Catholics who are in "irregular situations", which refers to those who are currently divorced, remarried, or cohabiting. All three of these individual personal situations are not morally accepted by the Church, which would cause many Catholics to feel alienated by Church. Pope Francis, through his Apostolic Exhortation, *Amoris Laetitia*, has requested a new pastoral approach by bishops, priests, and parish ministers and the parish community to involve and integrate these Catholics who might have once felt abandoned by the Church. Pope Francis's pastoral care is centered on the virtue of mercy. He emphasizes this message in *Amoris Laetitia*, in the section entitled "The Discernment of 'Irregular' Situations" by writing,

> There are two ways of thinking which recur throughout the Church's history: casting off and reinstating. The Church's way, from the time of the Council of Jerusalem, has always been the way of Jesus, the way of mercy and reinstatement... The way of the Church is not to condemn anyone for ever; it is to pour out the balm of God's mercy on all those

who ask for it with a sincere heart... For true charity is always unmerited, unconditional and gratuitous. (FRANCISCUS 2016a, §296; FRANCISCUS 2015)

Pope Francis is adamant that the Church is not a place to condemn people but rather a place of compassion and mercy. Many Catholics in the world find themselves living in situations of divorce, remarriage, and cohabitation with no concrete plan of inclusion from their local parishes and Church community. Pope Francis has changed this with his new pastoral approach for Catholics in "irregular situations". He is aware that many Catholics are in situations that are vastly different, and that he makes it clear that neither the Synod on the Family nor his Apostolic Exhortation offer a new set of canonical rules for cohabiting, divorced, and remarried persons. (FRANCISCUS 2016a, §300). Instead, Pope Francis calls for discernment. He writes, "what is possible is simply a renewed encouragement to undertake a responsible personal and pastoral discernment of particular cases, one which would recognize that, since 'the degree of responsibility is not equal in all cases' (SYNOD OF BISHOPS 2015, §51), the consequences or effects of a rule need not necessarily always be the same."[1] Therefore, the change happening with regard to the Church's approach to cohabiting, divorced, and remarried Catholics is not a doctrinal one that impacts canon law but a pastoral change that allows for lay and priestly discernment at the local level of the parish. Quoting the Synod of Bishops, Pope Francis writes in paragraph 300 in *Amoris Laetitia*,

> What we are speaking of is a process of accompaniment and discernment which 'guides the faithful to an awareness of their situation before God. Conversation with the priest, in the internal forum, contributes to the formation of a correct judgment on what hinders the possibility of a fuller participation in the life of the Church and on what steps can foster it and make it grow. Given that gradualness is not in the law itself (cf. *Familiaris Consortio*, 34), this discernment can never prescind from the Gospel demands of truth and charity, as proposed by the Church. For this discernment to happen, the following conditions must necessarily be present: humility, discretion and love for the Church and her teaching, in a sincere search for God's will and a desire to make a more perfect response to it'. (FRANCISCUS 2016a, §300; SYNOD OF BISHOPS, 2015, §86)[2]

Pope Francis is very clear concerning the process of accompaniment and discernment. He offers Catholics the opportunity for real discernment, with love, humility, and care, which must be done with gradualness. The point of gradualness is seen further in Pope Francis's remarks in *Amoris Laetitia* in paragraphs 293 through 295 in the section entitled, "Gradualness in Pastoral Care". In paragraph 295, Pope Francis remarks.

Along these lines, Saint John Paul II proposed the so-called 'law of gradualness' in the knowledge that the human being 'knows, loves and accomplishes moral good by different stages of growth.' (IOANNIS PAULI 1981, §34; IOANNIS PAULI 1982) This is not a 'gradualness of law' but rather a gradualness in the prudential exercises of free acts on the part of subjects who are not in a position to understand, appreciate, or fully carry out the objective demands of the law (FRANCISCUS 2016a, §295).

Throughout *Amoris Laetitia*, Pope Francis insists that the Church is not a Church which should judge or condemn, but instead be a merciful Church and show mercy towards those who are in situations which require pastoral care, especially those who are divorced, remarried, and cohabiting. He advocates using the virtue of mercy as a tool to help Catholics and not as a way of punishing or condemning them. Mercy is therefore the keystone in Pope Francis's new approach of pastoral care for these Catholics. In the Pope's most recent Apostolic Letter, *Misericordia et Misera*, Pope Francis offers a detailed understanding and description of God's mercy and what mercy entails. The Pope's

---

[1] *Amoris Laetitia*, §300.
[2] Ibid., §300; The Synod of Bishops, *Relatio Finalis*, October 24, 2015, http://www.vatican.va/roman_curia/synod/documents/rc_synod_doc_20151026_relazione-finale-xiv-assemblea_en.html, §85, accessed on 2 June 2017.

description offers Catholics, a greater understanding of two things. First, it offers Catholics an account of the biblical and theological definition of mercy, and second it gives a clearer idea of what Pope Francis envisions when he discusses mercy in his new pastoral approach for Catholics in "irregular situations" discussed in *Amoris Laetitia*. In *Misericordia et Misera*, Pope Francis writes,

> Nothing of what a repentant sinner places before God's mercy can be excluded from the embrace of his forgiveness. For this reason, none of us has the right to make forgiveness conditional. Mercy is always a gratuitous act of our heavenly Father, an unconditional and unmerited act of love. (FRANCISCUS 2016b, §2)

Pope Francis is clear that forgiveness and mercy can never be conditional. Therefore, the dioceses and parish communities helping Catholics in "irregular situations" cannot use mercy as a *quid pro quo* approach when caring for these persons. What I mean by this, is that priests and parish communities cannot use mercy as an exchange or a favour granted in return for something from Catholics in "irregular situations" i.e., to separate from a partner (cohabiting or married). Mercy is not conditional. He continues, "the experience of mercy enables us to regard all human problems from the standpoint of God's love, which never tires of welcoming and accompanying" (FRANCISCUS 2016b, § 14). Mercy is something that is to be celebrated, and the experience of mercy brings joy (ibid.). This is the message of the Gospel. Pope Francis's theology of mercy from this apostolic letter is inspiring because it describes God's mercy as a mercy which is not limited to certain moral situations. Mercy can be for all persons, including those in "irregular situations". The foundation of mercy always stays constant and always includes love since mercy involves compassion, which derives from God, who is all-loving. Forgiveness and repentance are also consistently connected to the virtue mercy. Pope Francis makes many comments concerning the "repentant sinner" and the weakness of situations of sin, in his Apostolic Letter, and so mercy cannot be understood without these elements of forgiveness and repentance. Therefore, Pope Francis is clear that mercy is the key to welcoming those Catholics in "irregular situations" back into the Church and sacraments (FRANCISCUS 2016a, footnote 351). This is visible in paragraphs 310 through 312 of *Amoris Laetitia* when Pope Francis comments on approaching these "irregular situations" (FRANCISCUS 2016a, §310–12). Pope Francis's pastoral approach of mercy will allow Catholics from unique situations to feel included and a part of their Church community. I value this approach because Pope Francis is adamant that mercy cannot be made conditional (ibid., §311–12. By not making mercy conditional, it allows a true sense of compassion that is to remain concrete and truly significant throughout all situations (ibid.; FRANCISCUS 2016b, §2). Mercy is not to be mistaken for a change in the Church's tradition regarding matters in sexual ethics. Instead, his approach is full of pastoral understanding and free from judgment and critical condemnation.

With all of this in mind, the question arises, how can Catholics practically implement this new approach to mercy that Pope Francis suggests? The answer to this question is currently being debated by many Catholic bishops and lay persons across the world. For example, Archbishop Charles J. Chaput of the Archdiocese of Philadelphia in the United States of America has published his own guidelines for the how the archdiocese is to understand and implement Pope Francis's remarks concerning "irregular situations" in *Amoris Laetitia* (Chaput 2016). I believe this new approach can be discussed with the use of Selling's method of the "virtuous trapezium" and revisiting the foundation of how Catholics are to think of and perceive the virtues. Mercy is a virtue, and by using Selling's method, Catholics can focus on how to understand mercy in their own individual context and circumstance, along with its complementary virtue (which would be punishment or restitution), rather than mercy as a perceived virtue on a pedestal, which one is supposed to live up to. Pope Francis's approach of mercy addresses a universal audience of many living in different circumstances. Selling's method does the same. Selling's method can be applied to an individual Catholic in a distinct context, and that is also the goal of Pope Francis's discussion on mercy in *Amoris Laetitia*. I will now further explain how Selling's method could be used to implement Pope Francis's approach of mercy.

4. Using Selling's Virtuous Trapezium Approach to Implement Pope Francis's Concept of Mercy for Catholics in "Irregular Situations"

Catholics across the world can use Selling's approach and method of the "virtuous trapezium" as a tool to implement mercy and the merciful tone Pope Francis discussed with his pastoral approach to persons in "irregular situations". In this section of the article, I give a real-life example of how Pope Francis's new pastoral approach of mercy can be seen and understood using Selling's approach to virtue. I suggest virtues be regarded not as isolated, individual entities that Catholics are supposed to live up to, but prompts—in Selling's words—"to formulate a certain way to respond to specific, challenging situations" (Selling 2016, p. 158). This can be connected to Pope Francis's discussion of discernment in *Amoris Laetitia*.

In the section in *Amoris Latitia*, under the headline, "Rules and Discernment", Pope Francis discusses the importance of practical discernment. He writes,

> Discernment must help to find possible ways of responding to God and growing in the midst of limits. By thinking that everything is black and white, we sometimes close off the way of grace and of growth, and discourage paths of sanctification which give glory to God. (FRANCISCUS 2016a, §305)

Pope Francis encourages Catholics to become active discerners in their daily lives. This is one of the reasons why I believe Selling's virtuous trapezium is a good concept when thinking about how to actualize Pope Francis's call for mercy concerning persons in "irregular situations". Here is another example of using the virtuous trapezium (see Figure 2). The complementary virtues you see are forgiveness/mercy and punishment/restitution. The extremes of these complementary virtues are placability and vengeance. The real-life situation which demands attention in this trapezium is "attitude towards wrong-doers". For the topic of this article, the phrase in the middle of that trapezium is the real life situation that Pope Francis is asking us to ethically address with mercy. This is where I believe Selling's method and approach to virtues can be used as a tool to actualize Pope Francis's pastoral approach into action. I will give an example, which might help bring this even more into perspective.

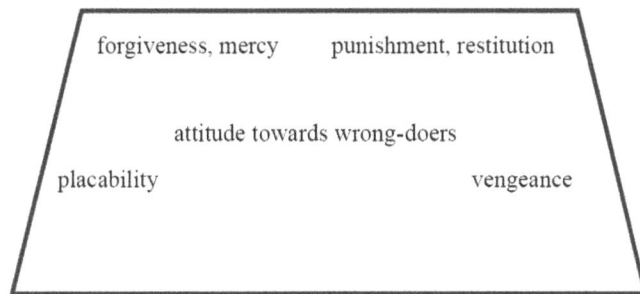

Figure 2. Forgiveness and Restitution Virtuous Trapezium (See Selling 2016, p. 234).

There are many Catholic couples who have married outside of the Catholic Church and want to belong and be a part of the Church, but since they did not follow the Catholic tradition of marriage, they feel excluded for many reasons. A couple that has married outside the Church and wants to be a part of the Church community should be able to do so with the help of pastoral discernment of their parish priest, thanks to this new Exhortation by Pope Francis. An entire outline of Pope Francis's pastoral suggestions on the issue of "irregular situations" can be found between paragraphs 296 through 312 of *Amoris Laetitia*. In this section of the document, Pope Francis asserts that the Church is a place of mercy and forgiveness and not a place which condemns anyone forever. In terms of pastoral solutions Pope Francis was very clear when it came to cohabiting couples, which I have mentioned above in section three of this article. In terms of the pastoral suggestions for couples that are remarried, the Pope suggests a careful examination and acknowledgement of complex situations where children are involved. Although a remarriage without an annulment is not ideal for the Church, the Synod Fathers state that careful discernment by pastors needs to take place, and an adequate approach which is appropriate for each individual situation is to be examined (FRANCISCUS 2016a, §298). Pope Francis takes this a step further and says, "I am in agreement with the many Synod Fathers who observed that 'the baptized who are divorced and civilly remarried need to be more fully integrated into Christian communities in the variety of ways possible, while avoiding any occasion of scandal.'" (ibid., §299). Pope Francis argues that the integration of these Catholics is the key to their pastoral care (ibid.). This integration is also extended to the children of these relationships. Overall, Pope Francis would like a renewed support for the pastoral and personal discernment of particular cases of persons in irregular situations (ibid., §300). I believe this is a great first step.

Pope Francis is advocating a merciful approach for Catholics in "irregular situations". Discerning how to fully actualise Pope Francis's approach will take careful consideration. This is where I believe Joseph Selling's model of the "virtuous trapezium" is helpful. Mercy does not simply mean tolerance, and that is illustrated within the trapezium figure above. Through Selling's model, we see the virtue of mercy in a continuum, and it is constantly being pulled in two directions between the complementary virtues. Therefore, the pastoral approach with mercy in pastoral discernment includes forgiveness, but in terms of what Pope Francis is saying for Catholics in "irregular situations", it does not mean that the Catholic Church endorses or promotes civil marriage for Catholics or remarriage or cohabitation for couples in irregular situations. There are many different factors at play here, which are illustrated by Selling's model itself, and this is another reason why I believe his method is a tool that Catholics can use to implement Pope Francis's approach for Catholics in "irregular situations". It is important here to take a step back and acknowledge that the Church is not changing its canonical laws on marriage or cohabitation. The church's expectations concerning marriage remain intact. What is different here is the recognition of a couple for whom living up to those expectations is not possible.

Selling's virtuous trapezium is the appropriate and current approach that can help Catholics discern Pope Francis's approach to mercy in matters of sexual ethics, and it is for that reason why I believe it is an important concept to discuss. However, in order to illustrate Selling's trapezium correctly, the complementary virtues of mercy need to be addressed within the picture of this discussion. Punishment and restitution are directly across from mercy and forgiveness in Selling's "virtuous trapezium". These are complementary virtues. Therefore, punishment and restitution are not to be ignored when using Selling's trapezium as a tool to actualize Pope Francis's approach of mercy into action. Focusing, for example, on the issue of pastoral and personal discernment in mercy of divorced persons in the Church, Selling would argue that there must be another conversation or action taking place which holds the parties accountable in some capacity. According to Selling, something must be done when one violates the expectations of the community or does not follow the "normal path" of dealing with, e.g., marital breakdown. Ordinarily, the church recommends seeking an annulment. Going through that process involves a form of "restitution" in the sense of coming to grips with the breakdown itself. The question then might be asked, to what extent was this person co-responsible? This is a question which requires further pastoral discernment. Selling's method therefore must take into account all elements of the trapezium in order to be used effectively.

As I have said before, Joseph Selling and Pope Francis are very similar in their approaches to help the Church become less concerned with an act-centered morality and more concerned with the situations and the reality that everyday Catholics and non-Catholics find themselves living in. Pope Francis's message of mercy concerns seeking truth in the realness of people's lives. In an interview with Anthony Spadaro, Pope Francis touches upon this by saying,

> The church sometimes has locked itself up in small things, in small-minded rules. The most important thing is the first proclamation: Jesus Christ has saved you. And the ministers of

the church must be ministers of mercy above all. The confessor, for example, is always in
danger of being either too much of a rigorist or too lax. Neither is merciful, because neither
of them really takes responsibility for the person. The rigorist washes his hands so that
he leaves it to the commandment. The loose minister washes his hands by simply saying,
"This is not a sin" or something like that. In pastoral ministry we must accompany people,
and we must heal their wounds. (Anthony 2013)

Pope Francis is concerned with helping and healing people, rather than condemning and checking to see if they have followed the moral rules of the Church with due diligence. Joseph Selling is advocating the same message to a certain degree with his "virtuous trapezium" in his book. He writes, "The consensus we might hope to achieve would have to be about method: the way we go about considering and arriving at ethical judgments" (Selling 2016, p. 9). Selling is concerned with a goal-oriented approach to ethical living rather than a behavioral or act centered approach (ibid., pp. 11–12). Pope Francis echoes this sentiment in *Evangelii Gaudium* when he writes,

> Here I repeat for the entire Church what I have often said to the priests and laity of Buenos Aires: I prefer a Church which is bruised, hurting and dirty because it has been out on the streets, rather than a Church which is unhealthy from being confined and from clinging to its own security. I do not want a Church concerned with being at the centre and which then ends by being caught up in a web of obsessions and procedures. If something should rightly disturb us and trouble our consciences, it is the fact that so many of our brothers and sisters are living without the strength, light and consolation born of friendship with Jesus Christ, without a community of faith to support them, without meaning and a goal in life. More than by fear of going astray, my hope is that we will be moved by the fear of remaining shut up within structures which give us a false sense of security, within rules which make us harsh judges, within habits which make us feel safe, while at our door people are starving and Jesus does not tire of saying to us: "Give them something to eat" (*Mk* 6:37). (FRANCISCUS 2013, §49)

Pope Francis and Selling are not obsessed with the rules and procedures of the tradition on sexuality; rather, they are concerned about the reality of the situations which many people find themselves in. Pope Francis and Selling are pursuing a way for people who have felt excluded or alienated by the Church, to address their situations through mercy and through their unique individual experiences. This message by both Selling and Pope Francis reaches out to Catholics (and non-Catholics) across different nations, cultures, races, genders, and social, economic and political situations. Selling's model of the "virtuous trapezium" is therefore a solid approach to address Pope Francis's message of mercy to matters of sexual ethics.

Further Considerations

I would like to propose a few further considerations on using Selling's model of the virtuous trapezium as a tool to actualize Pope Francis's provision of mercy to matters of sexual ethics. I think it is important to point out that not all Catholics agree that certain acts are sinful. For example, not all Catholics believe cohabitation or sexual intercourse before marriage are sinful acts. Therefore, for these Catholics, their discernment might be different than others that believe the opposite. However, does that make their discernment any less credible or plausible? Also, since many Catholic couples today are cohabiting before getting married, and many of these couples are then married in the Church, does that then mean that many parish priests are already actively discerning a merciful approach toward these couples? (O'Loughlin 2017) These are on-going questions to consider in my current research in how to understand Pope Francis's approach to discernment and pastoral approach of mercy to matters of sexual ethics while using Selling's approach and method of the virtuous trapezium as a tool to actualize Pope Francis's message. It is important to point out that these questions also concern a larger issue which considers if there are alternative approaches to dealing with questions in sexual ethics. I believe there are alternative approaches, but that is another conversation entirely.

5. Conclusions

I believe that Joseph Selling's method and approach to ethical living through his method of the "virtuous trapezium" can help Catholics apply what Pope Francis has said about mercy to matters of "irregular situations". Pope Francis's pastoral change, which advocates for lay and priestly discernment as well as a merciful approach toward persons in irregular situations, connects to Selling's idea of avoiding extremes when understanding virtues. I believe that Selling's method should be explored by moral theologians in the future because I believe it is an essential tool for further exploration and real dialogue within theological ethics in the twenty-first century.

Acknowledgments: The author would like to thank Heythrop College (London, England) and Anna Abram for inviting her to speak at The Future of Catholic Theological Ethics conference in January 2017 as well as Joseph Selling for his ground-breaking book which inspired this article. The author would also like to thank her Ph.D. supervisor, Julie Clague for her support and review of this article.

Conflicts of Interest: The author declares no conflict of interest.

References

Anthony, Spadaro. 2013. Interview with Pope Francis. August 19. Available online: https://w2.vatican.va/content/francesco/en/speeches/2013/september/documents/papa-francesco_20130921_intervista-spadaro.html (accessed on 30 April 2016).

Chaput, Charles J. 2016. Pastoral Guidelines for Implementing *Amoris Laetitia*. July 1. Available online: http://archphila.org/wp-content/uploads/2016/06/AOP_AL-guidelines.png (accessed on 4 June 2017).

FRANCISCUS, I. 2013. *Evangelii Gaudium*. November 24. Available online: http://w2.vatican.va/content/francesco/en/apost_exhortations/documents/papa-francesco_esortazione-ap_20131124_evangelii-gaudium.html (accessed on 30 April 2017).

SYNOD OF BISHOPS. 2015. Relatio Finalis, the Final Report of the Synod of Bishops to the Holy Father, Pope Francis. October 24. Available online: http://www.vatican.va/roman_curia/synod/documents/rc_synod_doc_20151026_relazione-finale-xiv-assemblea_en.html (accessed on 27 April 2017).

FRANCISCUS, I. 2015. Homily at Mass Celebrated with the New Cardinals. Available online: https://w2.vatican.va/content/francesco/en/homilies/2015/documents/papa-francesco_20150215_omelia-nuovi-cardinali.html (accessed on 27 November 2017).

FRANCISCUS, I. 2016a. *Amoris Laetitia*. Post-Synodal Exhortation. March 19. Available online: https://w2.vatican.va/content/dam/francesco/pdf/apost_exhortations/documents/papa-francesco_esortazione-ap_20160319_amoris-laetitia_en.png (accessed on 16 December 2016).

FRANCISCUS, I. 2016b. *Misericordia et Misera*. November 20. Available online: https://w2.vatican.va/content/francesco/en/apost_letters/documents/papa-francesco-lettera-ap_20161120_misericordia-et-misera.html (accessed on 23 December 2016).

IOANNIS PAULI, II. 1982. Acta Apostolicae Sedis. January 7. Available online: http://www.vatican.va/archive/aas/documents/AAS-74-1982-ocr.png (accessed on 4 June 2017).

IOANNIS PAULI, II. 1981. *Familiaris Consortio*. November 22. Available online: http://w2.vatican.va/content/john-paul-ii/en/apost_exhortations/documents/hf_jp-ii_exh_19811122_familiaris-consortio.html (accessed on 3 June 2017).

Selling, Joseph. 2016. *Reframing Catholic Theological Ethics*. Oxford: Oxford University Press.

O'Loughlin, Michael. 2017. Many Couples are Living Together before Marriage: What's the Church to Do? Available online: https://cruxnow.com/life/2014/09/29/more-couples-are-living-together-before-marriage-whats-the-church-to-do/ (accessed on 13 January 2016).

© 2017 by the author. Licensee MDPI, Basel, Switzerland. This article is an open access article distributed under the terms and conditions of the Creative Commons Attribution (CC BY) license (http://creativecommons.org/licenses/by/4.0/).

Article

Normative Virtue Theory in Theological Ethics

Nicholas Austin

Heythrop College, University of London, Kensington Square, London W8 5HQ, UK; n.austin@heythrop.ac.uk

Received: 17 August 2017; Accepted: 18 September 2017; Published: 29 September 2017

Abstract: What place is there for virtue theory in theological ethics? Many question the normative significance of virtue theory in theological ethics today, leaving it to rule-based ethics to provide action-guidance. There are three key objections to the normativity of virtue theory: that virtue theory is about agents rather than actions, that virtue theory has nothing to say directly about the morality of actions, and that the virtues are too vague to be of normative or action-guiding significance. This essay, drawing on Thomas Aquinas's account of virtue, challenges these perceptions and argues for a genuinely normative, action-guiding virtue theory within theological ethics. Theological ethics, in turn, can contribute to virtue theory, especially by its emphasis on the ecstatic nature of mature moral virtue, and through its reflection on the virtue of spiritual discernment.

Keywords: virtue ethics; virtue theory; theological ethics; Thomas Aquinas; normative ethics

1. Introduction

Joseph Selling's *Reframing Catholic Theological Ethics* helpfully addresses what is sometimes called "Fundamental Moral Theology," the part of theological ethics that deals with the more foundational questions to do with method, law, virtue, conscience, and moral action (Selling 2016). Selling combines study of the moral theological tradition—especially through an analysis of the ethics of Thomas Aquinas (1224–1274), and a critique of his interpreters such as Cardinal Cajetan (also known as Tommaso De Vio) (1468–1534)—with engagement with contemporary ethics. Here, I would like to focus on one topic in foundational theological ethics to which Selling attends, namely, virtue, and its role in theological reflection on morals. What is at stake here is not merely what theological ethics can contribute to the understanding of virtue, but also what virtue theory can offer theological ethics.

The widespread adoption of virtue theory by Catholic moralists can be understood, at least in part, as a response to the weaknesses of the sin-focused manuals of moral theology.[1] Catholic theological ethics, as is well known, has long been attempting to move beyond an atomistic focus on actions, that is, a distorting and blinkered concentration on individual acts divorced from the narrative of a person's life and the interior dispositions that are at the root of moral agency.(Mahoney 1987, pp. 1–36; Keenan 2008, pp. 9–34) Liberated by virtue theory, theological ethics, it is argued, can now confidently focus on the kind of persons we are called to become, rather than on parsing the species of mortal and venial sin.[2] Yet, as is often the case, the corrective risks introducing its own imbalance. An approach that recommends exclusive focus on one's own virtue seems peculiarly self-centered for an ethical theory, especially one informed by the New Testament vision of selfless love. Moreover, there is the danger that a one-sided focus on the character of the moral agent fails to say anything meaningful about moral behavior itself. Virtue theory, it may be objected, defaults on the obligation incumbent on ethicists to offer normative guidance.

---

[1] On virtue in contemporary Catholic theological ethics, see David Cloutier and William C. Mattison III, "Review Essay: The Resurgence of Virtue in Recent Moral Theology" (Cloutier and Mattison 2014).

[2] For a recent argument that virtue ethics represents the best approach to theological ethics today, see Michael G. Lawler and Todd A. Salzman, "Virtue Ethics: Natural and Christian," (Lawler and Salzman 2013).

Joseph Selling unwittingly adds fuel to this objection when he distinguishes in his book between "normative ethics", which is about applying rules to behavior, and "goal-centered ethics", which is about virtues and intentions (Selling 2016, pp. 10–12). This division-of-labor approach seems to suggest that all the renewal of virtue amounts to is an additional chapter in the moral textbooks, one that focuses on character, leaving it to other, rule-based chapters to deal with action and behavior. Yet, at the conclusion of his book, Selling holds open the possibility of a "convergence" between normative ethics and the more goal-centered, virtue-focused approach, into a "single method of ethical evaluation". He suggests, then, that a division of labor between the normative (that is, action guiding) aspects of theological ethics and virtue theory is based on a misguided dichotomy, and that their unification can result in "a fresh narrative about ethical living" (Selling 2016, p. 200). This is the suggestive insight that I would like to explore and develop, by defending more directly the normative significance of virtue theory within theological ethics. Virtue theory has the power to overcome the atomistic approach, not by shifting the focus, pendulum-like, from action to character, but rather by integrating reference to character into the moral evaluation of action.

If theological ethics needs virtue theory, does virtue theory need theological ethics? Today, there are many forms of virtue ethics other than the familiar neo-Aristotelian version (Carr et al. 2016). Like Selling, I take Thomas Aquinas's thinking about virtue to be an especially fruitful vein to mine, even in addressing contemporary questions in ethical theory, such as the relationship between the understanding of virtue and the resolution of particular moral decisions and issues. The riches of Aquinas's thinking about virtue arise, not merely from his often-perceptive reading of Aristotle, but also from particular emphases and insights from the theological tradition of which he is part. I shall attempt to point to theological resources integral to his ethics that help us form a more carefully calibrated account of the relationship of virtue theory and the ethical evaluation of action than is sometimes offered.

The argument for normative virtue theory will proceed by challenging what I perceive to be three common misconceptions about virtue theory: that virtue theory is about agents rather than actions, that virtue theory has nothing to directly say about the morality of actions, and that the virtues are too vague to be of normative or action-guiding significance.

2. Agents, Acts, and Ecstasy

The agent-focus of Aquinas's virtue theory is evident from his acceptance of the principle, *agere sequitur esse*, doing follows being.[3] This is the basis for Aquinas's focus on the virtues and vices, for, "being is prior by nature to acting".[4] While this principle is metaphysical in nature, Aquinas uses it to establish the necessity of the virtues:

> The manner of action follows the disposition of the agent, since as a thing is, such are the actions it works. And therefore, since virtue is the principle of some kind of operation, it is necessary that there pre-exist in the agent, according to virtue, some corresponding disposition.[5]

In other words, the virtues are necessary precisely because to live justly, mercifully, and patiently, one needs to be just, merciful, and patient. If, as ethicists, we are interested in good and bad actions, we should therefore be interested in their principles in the disposition of the agent's mind, will, and emotions.

---

[3] *Commentary on the Sentences*, lib. 3 d. 3 q. 2 a. 1 co: "agere sequitur ad esse perfectum, cum unumquodque agat secundum quod est in actu." Also *Summa Contra Gentiles*, lib. 3 cap. 69 n. 20: "agere sequitur ad esse in actu." For Aquinas's texts, I have relied on *Corpus Thomisticum. S. Thomae de Aquino Opera Omnia*. Edited by Enrique Alarcón. Pamplona, 2000. Online at http://www.corpusthomisticum.org/iopera.html. Translations are my own.

[4] *Summa Theologiae* (III 34.2 ad 1): "esse est prius natura quam agere."

[5] *Summa Theologiae* (I.II 55.2 ad 1).

However, for this very reason, Aquinas cannot be described as proposing an agent—*rather than act*—centered ethics. If we need the virtues precisely as principles of operation, then operation is also important, as their final cause. Activity is that for the sake of which virtue exists.

The act-orientation of Aquinas's virtue theory is evident in the important final-causal axiom, "every being exists for the sake of its operation".[6] Again, this is a metaphysical principle intended to apply universally to all created beings; yet, once again, it has significant implications in ethics. Aquinas deduces from this axiom that, in the case of the human person, it is precisely through operation, rather than merely habit, that the human person reaches her end.[7] In Aquinas's technical language, the first actuality (habit), as incomplete, exists *for the sake of* second actuality (activity), the more complete,[8] just as the musician's art exists for the sake of playing (and the goods that follow upon playing). The underlying metaphysics is one in which a substance, like a human being, reaches its fullest state of actualization precisely in operation, in activity. As Cajetan explains, "To say, 'Each being having an operation exists for the sake of its operation,' is to say nothing other than that it exists *for the sake of itself in complete and perfect actuality*".[9] (Emphasis added.)

This principle makes for a dynamic, rather than static virtue theory. Sometimes, virtue ethicists make it sound as though the ethical aim is to become virtuous. For example, one common way of explaining virtue ethics is that it asks three questions: "Who am I?" "Who should I become?" "How do I get there?" (Kotva 1996, p. 22) However, for Aquinas, the end of life is not a habit, but an activity; hence, virtue by itself cannot be the goal of life but only what orients us to that end. Following Aristotle, he notes that virtue does not lead to felicity if one lacks the opportunity to exercise it, or if one is asleep![10] The end of life is not merely to become good, but to become good-in-action.

The primacy of activity in Aquinas's virtue theory is seen also in his striking claim that, while in a certain sense virtue is better than an action, since it potentially or virtually contains within itself many good actions, strictly speaking a good act is better than the corresponding virtue.[11] He gives two reasons: first, it is better to act well than to be able to act well; and secondly, the goodness of a virtue derives entirely from its being an inclination to a good act, which is therefore more foundational. In sum, then, "operation according to virtue is more perfect than virtue itself".[12] Aquinas's virtue theory, then, is act-oriented in that operation is recognized as the final cause of virtue.[13]

So far, so philosophical. However, an underlying theological commitment is discernible in the way Aquinas sees virtue as referring, ultimately, not merely to the agent or the act, but beyond both. For the story of final causality does not stop with the act itself. Aquinas makes a distinction between two kinds of end, or rather, two aspects of any end: "the end is said in two ways: namely, the thing itself [*ipsa res*] that we desire to attain, and the use, namely, the attainment or possession of that thing".[14] In other words, there is the end as what ultimately is to be attained and as its very attainment. Does, then, the foundational axiom, "each thing exists for the sake of its operation," say that virtuous activity is the ultimate terminus of virtuous desire, that is, the thing itself that is desired, or merely the attainment of some further end? Cajetan offers the following answer:

---

[6] *On the Virtues* (1.9c): "omnis res est propter suam operationem." See especially *Summa Theologiae* I 105.5c, but also I 65.2c; 73.1.c; I.II 3.2.c; 49.3c ad 3 and 4 ad 1; II.II 9.1.c and ad 1; 32.4c.
[7] *Summa Theologiae* I.II 3.2c.
[8] *Summa Theologiae* I 105.5c.
[9] Cajetan (Tommaso de Vio), "Commentary on the Summa Theologiae," in *Sancti Thomae de Aquinas Opera Omnia Iussu Impensaque Leonis XIII*, vol. 6. (Rome: Editori di San Tommaso, 1882), p. 30: "Ita quod unumquodque habens operationem esse propter suam operationem, nihil aliud est quam esse propter seipsum in actu completo et perfecto." Notwithstanding the criticisms of Cajetan by Selling and others, I take it as obvious that his classic commentary on the *Summa Theologiae* can often be enlightening.
[10] *Commentary on the Ethics*, lib. 1 l. 5 n. 13.; *On the Virtues* (1.1 ad 4).
[11] *Summa Theologiae* I.II 71.3c and ad 1.
[12] *Commentary on the Ethics*, lib. 1 l. 12 n. 14.
[13] See also the helpful discussion in David A. Horner, "Is Aquinas an Act-Ethicist or an Agent-Ethicist?" (Horner 2006).
[14] *Summa Theologiae* I.II 2.7c.

"[E]ach thing exists on account of its operation" could mean two things. First, it could mean that each thing exists for its operation as the thing that is the end; and thus it is completely false [*falsissimum*]. Secondly, it could mean that each thing exists for its operation as its proper complement; and, in this sense, it is true.[15]

Cajetan's point is that operation is not the thing itself [*ipsa res*] that is desired: the operations of knowing and loving are only the end as the attainment of some further end, not the ultimate end itself, the object that is known and loved. As Aquinas puts it, the end, the thing itself to be attained, that in which beatitude lies, exists "outside of the soul", *extra animam*.[16]

This has important implications. Admittedly, virtue theory will focus primarily on the virtues and their role in human life. However, virtue theory should not recommend the attainment of virtue, or even virtuous activity, as the primary ethical motivation or point of moral attention, since that would be to fall into a narcissistic moral perfectionism. As theological ethicist William Spohn suggests, "The virtuous life shifts attention from personal perfection to more important concerns" (Spohn 1999, p. 13). Similarly, philosopher Christine Swanton notes that it is right to have a "background desire" to be virtuous, but that virtuous people have as "foreground motivations" such things as desires to help friends for their own sakes (Swanton 2003, p. 29). While a desire to grow in virtue is one commendable aspiration among others, we should not fixate on how virtuous we are becoming, as though every morning we should get up and weigh ourselves on the scale of virtue and vice to see how well we have progressed, or how badly we have regressed. Such moral obsession is neither praiseworthy nor, ironically, is it the path to virtue.

Aquinas rightly denies, then, that the overriding, foreground motivation should be to possess the virtues, or even to live virtuously. His reasons for denying this are theological as well as philosophical, having to do with the Christian understanding of the virtue of love or charity, *caritas*. Aquinas distinguishes four levels or grades of possession of this virtue, according to the focus of a person's *studium*, her striving and attention. Beginners focus on avoiding sin; those who are progressing do principally attend to increasing in the virtue of love; but the advanced, in a scriptural phrase, "desire to be dissolved and to be with Christ".[17] Finally, in heaven, "the whole heart of a human person is always actually borne towards God".[18] As with all developmental models, these stages should not be taken too schematically. However, the model does show that, for Aquinas, growth in virtue shifts the focus from self to the other: the end-point and perfection of virtue is self-forgetfulness and being "always actually borne towards God". As Aquinas explains elsewhere:

> It is necessary for the perfection of charity not only to abandon exterior things, but even in some way to abandon oneself. For [Pseudo-]Dionysius says (*On the Divine Names*, Ch. 4), that "divine love produces ecstasy", that is, it places a human being outside himself, not allowing a human to be for his own self, but for the beloved.[19]

Aquinas's theological, developmental virtue theory recommends an attentiveness and desire that grows from being *act*-focused to being also *agent*-focused, and finally to being *other*-focused. What Aquinas proposes, in the end, is an ecstatic virtue theory.

This reading of Aquinas and Cajetan suggests that to say that virtue theory is necessarily agent-centered rather than act-centered is an over-simplification bordering on a misrepresentation. To focus on the virtues is indeed to concentrate on the being of the agent. Yet, the virtues are by nature oriented to act as to their end or final cause, that for the sake of which they have their being. Just as

---

[15] Cajetan, Ibid., p. 30.
[16] *Summa Theolgoiae* I.II 2.7c.
[17] *Summa Theologiae* II.II 24.9c. Cf. Philippians 1:23.
[18] *Summa Theologiae* II.II 24.8c.
[19] *De perfectione*, cap. 10 co. (cf. *Summa Theologiae* I.II 28.3.)

reference to an object is integral to a transitive verb, so reference to act is integral to virtue.[20] And so virtue theory is also act-focused, insofar as it concerns habits that are, by their very essence, principles of virtuous operation. Finally, it helps, with Jorge Garcia, to make an important distinction: "Virtues may be seen as the proper focus of the *moral subject's* attention, or, alternatively, it can be claimed that virtues are the proper focus of the *moral theorist's* attention" (Garcia 2010). On my reading, while virtue theory does legitimately focus its own attention on virtue, it does not recommend virtue as the overriding focus of attention for the moral subject. At most, moral subjects have a helpful background desire for virtue. A theological virtue theory, because of its understanding of the nature of theological love, is in a good position to recognize that the loving, compassionate, and just person is not focused primarily on her own moral state, but is self-forgetfully or "ecstatically" concerned with the other to whom love, compassion, or justice are due.

3. Virtue Theory and the Moral Evaluation of Actions

The moral manuals of Catholic moral theology, for all their faults, did manage to say a lot about which kinds of action were right, and which were wrong. Selling, while wanting to put some water between his own approach and that of the moral manuals, nevertheless recognizes the danger of an overcorrection that abandons the important task of evaluating specific behaviors (Selling 2016, p. 200). For some, however, virtue theory is impotent to contribute towards this important task. As Robert Louden puts it, "What sets [virtue ethics] apart from other approaches, again, is its strong agent orientation. So for virtue ethics, the primary object of moral evaluation is not the act or its consequences, but rather the agent" (Louden 1984, p. 228).

To begin to question this assertion, it helps to return to the paper widely credited as launching the return to virtue, Elizabeth Anscombe's, "Modern Moral Philosophy" of 1958 (Anscombe 1958). It is not always noticed that one of the primary reasons Anscombe advocates a recovery of the "thick" language of the virtues is precisely because our moral vocabulary for talking about the morality of *actions* had become too "thin". For her, it would be progress if, instead of labelling actions as "morally right" or "morally wrong", we named the kind or type of the action. When I challenge a friend for acting unjustly, I may do so lovingly, sensitively, wisely, and temperately; or alternatively, I may do so vengefully, insensitively, foolishly, and intemperately. Such moral descriptions of actions are clearly derived from virtue- and vice-terms. It is striking, then, that at the outset of the renewal of virtue, one of the primary reasons given for its return is precisely that virtue helps us to talk, not just about the character of the agent, but also about particular actions.

For confirmation that virtue theory has something to say about the ethics of actions, it helps, once again, to return to Aquinas. Aquinas offers an analysis of the morality of actions in the *Summa Theologiae*, when he comes to consider "the goodness and malice of human acts" (I.II 18 Pr). He approaches the topic through the question of "specification". Each particular deliberate action is either good or evil in its species (I.II 18.9). The question, then, is how to determine the moral species of an action. As Joseph Pilsner explains, "In moral theory, identifying a human action's kind is of considerable importance. Although in some instances making such a determination is relatively easy—it doesn't take a trained moralist to recognize flagrant cases of murder, stealing, or adultery—in other instances, the task can be a challenge" (Joseph 2006, p. 1). For Pilsner, this challenge is met by Aquinas's theory of moral action, insofar as he identifies the determinants of the moral species of a human action. However, while much ink has been spilled over the interpretation of Aquinas's theory of the specification of human actions in terms of their object, circumstances, and end, it is rarely explained what are the "species" or types of moral action to which he is referring. Because of Aquinas's tendency to abstract rigor, it is not easy to tell. In his treatise on the moral goodness and malice of human acts, Aquinas does offer a few examples: theft, adultery, almsgiving, vanity, and murder. From this list alone, we may be forgiven for assuming

---

[20] I thank an anonymous referee for this comparison.

that the vocabulary for describing moral character on the one hand, and moral action on the other, are disparate. However, Aquinas himself clearly sees an intimate connection. Theft and murder are acts of the vice of injustice; adultery expresses both unchastity and injustice; almsgiving is an act of the virtue of mercy; and vanity is referred back to vainglory, a vice opposed to magnanimity and humility. This helps to make sense of Aquinas's well-cited claim that "the whole subject-matter of morals may be reduced [*reducta*] to the consideration of the virtues" (I.II Pr.). Whatever moral descriptions we give of particular actions may be "reduced", that is "led back" to the language of virtues and vices.

Like Aquinas, a number of contemporary virtue theorists have stressed the relationship between the virtues and particular actions. They have done so primarily by offering a virtue-based answer to the question, "What makes a right action right, and a wrong action wrong?" For example, according to Rosalind Hursthouse, "An action is right iff it is what a virtuous agent would characteristically (i.e., acting in character) do in the circumstances" (Rosalind 1999). Such accounts have been criticized on various grounds. If a right action is what a virtuous person characteristically would do, then it can never be right to express contrition, or to seek to become a virtuous person, or ask for guidance from someone wiser than myself, or force myself to be self-controlled, since a virtuous person may never have to do these things (Johnson 2003). More promising is Jorge Garcia's approach, which eliminates any counterfactual reference to what the virtuous person would do. For him, "acting wrong is acting viciously, and ... we can understand someone's acting rightly (in the minimal sense of behaving permissibly) as conducting herself in a way that is not genuinely vicious in any way in the situation" (Garcia 2010, p. 106). Presumably, then to act rightly in the positive sense of doing morally well, is simply to act virtuously. To the objection that we judge actions as wrong (or right), not so much by using vice- and virtue-language, as by appealing to certain action descriptions, Garcia replies: "we notice that we typically judge these types of action wrong by linking them to vices (or, at least, to vicious inputs). Thus, we explain that stealing and murder are wrong in that they are unjust, that lying is immoral because dishonest, that torture is cruel, adultery disloyal, and other forms of behavior weak-willed, cowardly, inconsiderate, and so on ... [T]hese vice terms present the *way* in which each type of action is moral wrong" (Garcia 2010, p. 106). Like Aquinas, Garcia traces the moral descriptors of actions back to the language of the virtues and the vices. Virtue theory is therefore able to contend with consequentialist and deontological normative ethical theories in offering an account of morally right and wrong actions.

Far from having nothing to say about actions, therefore, it is to virtue theory that we need to look to provide the thick moral language that both describes individual actions, and, as Garcia argues, explains the *way* in which actions are right or wrong, morally good or bad. For this reason, theological ethics needs virtue theory, not merely to describe the character of the moral subject, but even to characterize her behaviors.

4. Virtue Theory, Action-Guidance, and Vagueness

It is often claimed that virtue theory is too vague to be of normative or action-guiding significance. Louden puts the objection as follows: "people have always expected ethical theory to tell them something about what they ought to do, and it seems to me that virtue ethics is structurally unable to say much of anything about this issue. If I'm right, one consequence of this is that a virtue-based ethics will be particularly weak in the areas of casuistry and applied ethics" (Louden 1984, p. 229). It is odd, however, that those who continue to object in this way do not advert to the increasingly vast literature applying virtue ethics to various issues and fields of practice.[21]

A defense of virtue theory's directive potential may begin with Hursthouse's observation that virtue theory provides what she calls v-rules: "not only does each virtue generate a prescription—act

---

[21] See, for example, Rebecca L. Walker and P. J. Ivanhoe, eds., *Working Virtue: Virtue Ethics and Contemporary Moral Problems* (Walker and Ivanhoe 2007).

honestly, charitably, justly—but each vice a prohibition—do not act dishonestly, uncharitably, unjustly" (Rosalind 2003, p. 190). There is, then, an implicit prescriptivity to the concepts of the virtues and the vices. Moreover, I believe that it is possible to improve upon Hursthouse's v-rules. I have argued elsewhere that, on one reading of Aquinas, a virtue can be analyzed according to a number of distinct elements (Austin 2017). Without going into the details of the theory, a rule such as "be temperate" can be unpacked into something like the following: "When faced with emotional attractions to food, drink, sex, consumer goods, etc., modulate those attractions to meet need rather than luxury (where 'need' refers to what is necessary to live a humanly fitting bodily, relational, and moral life), by restraining or positively rechanneling these desires through practices such as fasting and grateful enjoyment, thereby, even in one's appetites, following, dying, and rising with Christ". If we thinly characterize a virtue like temperance as something like "moderation", it will indeed be too vague to offer much normative guidance. Yet a thicker description, of the kind that Aquinas offers, implicitly contains a great deal of normative guidance. The v-rule, "Be temperate", warns us that there are certain characteristic objects in human life that elicit strong emotional attractions, which have the tendency to overrun their bounds and become destructive of the human good for self and others; that there is consequently a basic moral task in life to modulate these attractions in a way that contributes to a morally good, flourishing human life; that often this modulation will involve setting due limits, or redirecting one's attractions towards other objects; and that bodily practices such as fasting will often be necessary, although it is important also to avoid Manichaeism by finding a place for grateful celebration of the good gifts and pleasures God provides through his creation; and that this mortification and rising to new life of appetite is one aspect of a life patterned on Christ's. Virtue concepts are highly condensed packets of normativity, encoding a rich tradition of practical wisdom about how best to respond in some field of thinking, desiring, and acting. Through reflection on experience, we grow in the ability to recognize how the practical wisdom specific to each moral virtue is to be specified in concrete situations. The more deeply we understand the virtues, the more the v-rules, then, can guide us in how to live.

Garcia, like Hursthouse, connects virtue and moral rules, but in an even more integral way. He notes, following Henry Richardson, that norms should be formulated so that they are "transparent": "it is a desideratum of the formulation of any norm—that is, the statement of some obligation, permission, and the like—that it be transparent, making explicit on its face not just that some course of action is forbidden, but also why it is. This renders the norm more accessible, comprehensible, and open to our efforts at interpretation and justification" (Garcia 2010, p. 104). For Garcia, virtue- and vice-terms present the best candidates for making a norm transparent. Parents know this intuitively: "Be generous and share your sweets", "Don't shout, that's disrespectful", and so on. It is not merely, then, that virtue and vice terms generate v-rules or norms, but that moral norms themselves are best expressed in terms of virtues and vices, as they make moral rules "transparent". Once again, the dichotomy between normative ethics and virtue theory looks increasingly questionable.

It may be objected that, even given the guidance of v-rules, or rules formulated by reference to virtue- and vice terms, virtue theory of itself fails to provide us exact guidance on what we should do in concrete situations. When faced with a difficult dilemma, it is not always clear what is the virtuous thing to do. This objection may rest upon the illusory search for the perfect normative theory, one that provides a "decision procedure", able to tell us how to act rightly in any conceivable situation. Hursthouse asks a disarming question: Supposing a very clever teenager became proficient at applying such a normative theory, would you go to her for moral counsel (Rosalind 2003, p. 193)? That we would not is a sign that we know that moral wisdom about how to act in the concrete circumstances of a person's life cannot be reduced to mastery of an algorithm or rulebook. Ethical theory, we may hope, can serve in the cultivation of the virtue practical wisdom; it cannot bypass it in directing action here and now. At best, ethical theory is like a military strategist directing things from afar: whatever guidance it gives, it has to leave some space for the final judgement to the soldier on the ground.

The irreplaceability of the moral subject's judgement in concrete situations is also recognized by Aquinas:

> And since the discussion of morals even in general terms is uncertain and variable, it becomes yet more uncertain if someone wants to descend further [to particulars], offering teaching specifically about singulars. For this does not fall under art, or under any narration, because the cases of singular actions vary in infinitely many ways. And so the judgment about particulars is left to the prudence of each.[22]

This passage comes from Aquinas's *Commentary on the Nicomachean Ethics*, and so may seem merely to be the working out of a philosophical insight into the impossibility of a perfectly codified ethics. Yet, once again, it is possible to detect in Aquinas here his dependence, not just on the Philosopher, but on a more theological, spiritual tradition, in this case that of discernment or "discretion", stretching back to Gregory the Great, Augustine, and Cassian.[23] It is through discernment that one interiorly comes to understand and accept what God is asking one to do. Given the surprising and unpredictable nature of God's invitation in a particular human life—something with which Aquinas was intimately familiar, persisting in a vocation to Dominican religious life despite strong parental opposition—discernment of what ought to be done cannot always be reduced to the application of general rules to a particular circumstance (Endean 2004, pp. 106–11). It is therefore unsurprising that Pope Francis, in his Apostolic Exhortation, *Amoris Laetitia*, appeals both to Aquinas and the idea of discernment to avoid a reductive, rule-based approach to complex moral and pastoral questions: "It is reductive simply to consider whether or not an individual's actions correspond to a general law or rule, because that is not enough to discern and ensure full fidelity to God in the concrete life of a human being" (Pope Francis 2016). The spiritual tradition of discernment is a bulwark against an unduly legalistic or overly codified approach to moral decision making.

5. Conclusions

This essay, by taking Thomas Aquinas as a primary reference point, has attempted to delineate something of the contribution of virtue theory to theological, normative ethics, as well as the contribution of theological ethics to the theory of virtue. To see virtue theory as primarily focused on character is to underestimate the way virtue theory can assist theological ethics in its task of evaluating moral actions and thereby offering the right degree of action guidance, neither being too vague to be of any help, nor attempting to control what should be left to the prudential, discerning judgement of the situated moral subject. Theological ethics can warn virtue theory away from a narcissistic moral perfectionism by its insight into the ecstatic nature of fully mature virtue, as manifest most clearly in the theological virtue of love. A specifically theological ethics can also help to resist the misguided attempt at complete codifiability in moral decision making through its respect for the practice of spiritual discernment, which searches for knowledge of the ever-surprising will of God in the particularities of a person's life. Just as a genuinely normative virtue theory enriches theological ethics, so theological ethics may contribute to the theory of virtue.

Acknowledgments: This study was not funded. The author is grateful for reviewer comments on an earlier draft of this paper.

Conflicts of Interest: The author declares no conflict of interest.

References

Anscombe, Gertrude E. M. 1958. Modern Moral Philosophy. *Philosophy* 33: 1–19. [CrossRef]
Austin, Nicholas. 2017. *Aquinas on Virtue: A Causal Reading*. Moral Traditions Series; Washington: Georgetown University Press.

---

[22] *Commentary on the Ethics*, lib. 2 l. 2.5.
[23] On the history of discernment, see McIntosh, Mark, *Discernment and Truth: Meditations on the Christian Life of Contemplation and Truth* (McIntosh 2004).

David Carr, James Arthur, and Kristján Kristjánsson, eds. 2016. *Varieties of Virtue Ethics*. London: Palgrave Macmillan.
Cloutier, David, and William C. Mattison III. 2014. Review Essay: The Resurgence of Virtue in Recent Moral Theology. *Journal of Moral Theology* 3: 228–59. [CrossRef]
Endean, Philip. 2004. *Karl Rahner and Ignatian Spirituality*. Oxford: Oxford University Press.
Garcia, Jorge L. A. 2010. The Virtues of the Natural Moral Law. In *Natural Moral Law in Contemporary Society*. Edited by Holger Zaborowski. Washington: Catholic University of America Press, p. 101.
Horner, David A. 2006. Is Aquinas an Act-Ethicist or an Agent-Ethicist? *The Thomist* 70: 237–65. [CrossRef]
Rosalind, Hursthouse. 1999. *On Virtue Ethics*. Oxford: Oxford University Press.
Rosalind, Hursthouse. 2003. Normative Virtue Ethics. In *Virtue Ethics*. Edited by Stephen L. Darwall. Oxford: Wiley-Blackwell.
Johnson, Robert N. 2003. Virtue and Right. *Ethics* 113: 810–34. [CrossRef]
Keenan, James F. 2008. *A History of Catholic Moral Theology in the Twentieth Century: From Confessing Sins to Liberating Consciences*. London: Continuum.
Kotva, Joseph J. 1996. *The Christian Case for Virtue Ethics*. Washington: Georgetown University Press.
Lawler, Michael G., and Todd A. Salzman. 2013. Virtue Ethics: Natural and Christian. *Theological Studies* 74: 442–73. [CrossRef]
Louden, Robert B. 1984. On Some Vices of Virtue Ethics. *American Philosophical Quarterly* 21: 228–29.
Mahoney, John. 1987. *The Making of Moral Theology: A Study of the Roman Catholic Tradition. The Martin D'Arcy Memorial Lectures, 1981-2*. Oxford: Clarendon Press.
McIntosh, Mark. 2004. *Discernment and Truth: Meditations on the Christian Life of Contemplation and Truth*. New York: Crossroad.
Joseph, Pilsner. 2006. *The Specification of Human Actions in St. Thomas Aquinas*. Oxford: Oxford University Press.
Pope Francis. 2016. Amoris Laetitia. Available online: http://w2.vatican.va/content/francesco/en/apost_exhortations/documents/papa-francesco_esortazione-ap_20160319_amoris-laetitia.html (accessed on 19 March 2016).
Selling, Joseph A. 2016. *Reframing Catholic Theological Ethics*. Oxford: Oxford University Press.
Spohn, William C. 1999. *Go and Do Likewise: Jesus and Ethics*. New York: Continuum.
Swanton, Christine. 2003. *Virtue Ethics: A Pluralistic View*. New York: Oxford University Press.
Rebecca L. Walker, and P. J. Ivanhoe, eds. 2007. *Working Virtue: Virtue Ethics and Contemporary Moral Problems*. Oxford: Clarendon Press.

© 2017 by the author. Licensee MDPI, Basel, Switzerland. This article is an open access article distributed under the terms and conditions of the Creative Commons Attribution (CC BY) license (http://creativecommons.org/licenses/by/4.0/).

Article

Reframing Catholic Theological Ethics from a Scotistic Perspective

Nenad Polgar

Faculty of Catholic Theology, University of Vienna, Schenkenstraße 8-10, 1010 Vienna, Austria; nenad.polgar@univie.ac.at

Received: 17 August 2017; Accepted: 16 September 2017; Published: 21 September 2017

Abstract: The article engages with Joseph Selling's most recent publication *Reframing Catholic Theological Ethics* in which he invites theological ethicists to re-think the post-Tridentine development of theological ethics by noting its methodological deficiencies, misrepresentation of sources, and an insufficient interest in the most fundamental question: What is it that we are trying to achieve in our moral lives in the first place? In order to re-orient the discipline, Selling proposes a new reading of Thomas Aquinas' *Treatise on Human Acts* (ST I-II, 1-21), but the present author argues that this might not be enough, given the debate within the discipline on how Aquinas' text ought to be interpreted. Hence, the author proposes an alternative route to 'reframing Catholic theological ethics' via the works of John Duns Scotus and explores his ethical ideas that might be pertinent for such a project. The main focus of the article is a reflection on Scotus' 'case study' of marriage and bigamy in the Old Testament that justifies drawing a parallel between his work and Selling's attempt to reframe Catholic theological ethics.

Keywords: John Duns Scotus; theological ethics; marriage and bigamy; Thomas Aquinas; *recta ratio*

1. Introduction

In his most recent publication *Reframing Catholic Theological Ethics*, Joseph Selling invites us to re-think the post-Tridentine development of theological ethics. He argues that the excessive focus on the object of the act and a specific understanding of natural law have deformed the discipline and turned it into a confessional tool, rather than the specifically Christian way of engaging with and reflecting on moral life. Although he argues that such an approach was understandable and, perhaps, even necessary within that particular period of Church history, continuous insistence on it, even after the Second Vatican Council, is highly problematic. Namely, it misrepresents its own claimed sources (most notably, Thomas Aquinas) and misses the crucial insights that these tried to convey, is entirely oblivious of underlying methodological issues, and brought the whole discipline to a deadlock, to mention just a few (Selling 2016, pp. 1–12). In the effort to correct or, at least, prompt us to reflect on current deficiencies in the discipline of theological ethics, Joseph Selling proposes a different reading of Aquinas' *Treatise on Human Acts* (*Summa theologiae* I-II, qq. 1-21); one that would show a greater awareness of Thomas' overall aretaic approach and raise questions such as—what is it that we are trying to achieve in our moral lives in the first place (Selling 2016, chp. 3)?

Although there is much to commend in Selling's approach in general, one might expect that the reaction to his call within the professional community will depend very much on whether his interpretation of Aquinas will be accepted or at least engaged with. Unfortunately, Richard McCormick's comment that one can get almost anything out of Aquinas if enough texts are adduced (McCormick 1981, p. 67), works against Selling's interpretation, precisely because of the longstanding influence of manuals of moral theology. A possible way to deal with this problem would be to expand the basis on which Selling's argument rests and offer alternative routes to "reframing Catholic theological ethics". In that effort, this paper will briefly explore ethically relevant concepts of another medieval giant of theological thought, who has been relegated to the margins of the theological enterprise in manuals of moral theology, John Duns Scotus. More specifically, the goal of the paper is to try to justify using Scotus as a source for reframing theological ethics by offering a short introduction into his ethical thought and then reflecting on how he dealt with the concrete issue of marriage and bigamy. This will, finally, allow some parallels between Selling's and Scotus' approach to moral reasoning to be drawn—(1) the notion of premoral and moral good and evil; (2) the primary importance of the end in the specification and evaluation of moral acts; and (3) the (ir)relevancy of the concept of intrinsic evil. If demonstrated, the convergence between the two authors ought to recommend the need for a deeper engagement with Scotus' writings within the contemporary discipline of Catholic theological ethics as an inspiration for its renewal and a way around endless debates on the right interpretation of Aquinas.

2. Why Scotus?

There is much to commend Scotus' theology as a source for reframing Catholic theological ethics, but before I turn to it, I would like to comment briefly on his historical significance in relation to such a project. At first sight, it seems that Scotus' historical (in)significance argues against enlisting him as a source for reframing Catholic theological ethics. Namely, despite his early popularity which lasted until the seventeenth century and, according to some scholars, spawned a theological school that was perhaps even more influential than the Thomistic school (Osborne 2014, pp. xiv–xv), the more recent period has not been so kind to Scotus. This, of course, was due to two reasons; (1) a general impression that Scotus was an intellectual predecessor of William of Ockham[1]; and (2) the rise of and official support that Thomism received, especially after the promulgation of the encyclical *Aeterni patris* of Leo XIII (Leo 1879)[2]. Hence, one might argue, for better or for worse, Scotus has fallen out of favour with the more recent developments in moral theology and Aquinas carried the day.

Despite this unfortunate development, in my opinion, Scotus should not be treated as irrelevant or reduced to a theological footnote. On the contrary, this puts him and his theology in a unique position to contribute significantly to the renewal of theological ethics. As I pointed out earlier, his diminished authority is precisely what spared him Aquinas' fate of being re-interpreted by the manualists. True, theologians like Thomas de Vio (Cardinal Cajetan) and Francisco Suarez commented on and interpreted Scotus, but the scope of this is hardly comparable with the attention Aquinas received. For this reason, it is much easier and it invokes much less controversy to go back to his texts.

On the other hand, if there is any merit to Selling's position, it indicates that Thomas' understanding of ethics was disfigured and misunderstood during the manualist period and, therefore, one could argue that Thomas was the dominant authority during that period in name only. In other words, what was authoritative was a later interpretation of Thomas, while his original contribution has been pushed to the side, as much as Scotus' was, albeit for different reasons. Nevertheless, this will still cause significant, perhaps insurmountable, difficulties for any contemporary attempt at a retrieval of Thomas' actual position in *Summa theologiae* I-II, qq. 1–21 and this is why turning to Scotus can be an easier route for the renewal of theological ethics or at the very least, Selling might find in him a valuable ally for his project.

---

[1] Scotus' decline was, in my opinion, more a result of this general impression than respective differences between him and Aquinas, which is not to deny that there were differences between them. This general impression was that Scotus was a proponent of voluntarism, while Aquinas was a proponent of intellectualism and the latter was more in line with the Catholic understanding of morality. Although this observation rests on how Scotus was treated by theologians of the Second Scholasticism and the manual tradition within the Catholic Church, the Radical Orthodoxy movement has further fueled this skepticism towards Scotus in the recent decades. Cf. (Pickstock 2005, pp. 563–69).

[2] The subtitle of the encyclical letter, *On the Restoration of Christian Philosophy in Catholic Schools in the Spirit of the Angelic Doctor, St. Thomas Aquinas*, is very suggestive in terms of its aim.

3. Scotus' Meta-Ethics in a Nutshell

As a preliminary note, it is important to point out that on the meta-ethical level, Scotus aims at preserving both divine reason and freedom against what might be called the view of ancient Greek necessitarianism, i.e., the notion that everything truly real and worth knowing proceeds from the first necessary cause and, therefore, true knowledge consists of necessary truths, not contingent ones (Jaczn et al. 1994, pp. 18–19). Aquinas also subscribed to this view, but modified it in order to take into account the Christian doctrine of creation (Aquinas 1955–1957, b. II, chp. 30)[3]. Scotus, however, went a step further and posited that God did not only decide freely to create the world, but also decided freely what kind of world he will create, among many different possibilities imaginable (Jaczn et al. 1994, p. 90; Lectura b. 1, dist. 39, q. 5)[4]. This position introduces contingency into creation (and, implicitly, into the moral order) and ascribes it to the first cause, God.[5]

One of the consequences of this position is that Scotus' concept of natural law is more complex then Aquinas', insofar as it takes into account the contingency of the world and disassociates the goals and values we pursue from the ultimate end, the beatific vision of God. Some authors refer to this as Scotus' "denaturalisation" of the natural law, where the order of the precepts of the law of nature does not simply, as in Aquinas, follow the order of natural inclinations (Möhle 2003, p. 313)[6]. Instead, Scotus posits the distinction between natural law in the strict sense and natural law in the extended sense. The former refers to those precepts that are necessarily true, while the latter refers to those precepts which can be shown to be in harmony with the former, but not necessarily true. To illustrate this point, Scotus refers to the Decalogue and claims that only the commandments about loving God (first tablet) belong to the natural law in the strict sense, while all other commandments belong to the natural law in the extended sense (Wolter and Frank 1997, p. 195; *Ordinatio* b. IV, dist. 17). This will have far reaching consequences for his whole ethical theory. Furthermore, since Scotus refuses "a matrix in which our existence is completely fixed" (Jaczn et al. 1994, p. 22) and moral absolutes associated with commandments of the second tablet of the Decalogue, his ethical thought further substantiates Selling's call to rethink moral methodology.

4. Marriage and Bigamy

Perhaps the most illustrative example of the application of Scotus' ethical theory is his treatment of the Old Testament cases of divine dispensations. One such case concerns marriage and bigamy, and he asks the question: "So far as the Mosaic law or the law of nature is concerned, was bigamy ever licit or, were the patriarch of old allowed to have several wives joined in the bonds of matrimony?" (Wolter and Frank 1997, p. 208; *Ordinatio* b. IV, dist. 33, q. 1) In the continuation, Scotus first aims to establish the purposes of marriage and the status of the precept related to it as being a precept of natural law in the extended sense, in order to demonstrate that this issue qualifies as a candidate for

---

[3] References to Aquinas' translated works in the main text are specified by the modern edition, followed by details of the original work (title, book (b.), distinction (dist.), question (q.), or chapter (chp.)).

[4] References to Scotus' translated works in the main text are specified by the modern edition, followed by details of the original work (title, book (b.), distinction (dist.), question (q.), and article (a.)).

[5] Hence, one could say that Aquinas tried to justify the doctrine of creation within the frame of ancient Greek necessitarianism by introducing into it the act of creation, while Scotus found the view entirely incompatible with the doctrine of creation and developed an alternative ontology.

[6] In other words, Scotus does not follow the Thomistic understanding that links the eternal law with creation (including "nature" and natural inclinations) through the notion of natural law as a rational participation in the eternal law. In fact, the whole notion of eternal law has no role in his ethical system. Instead, what belongs to the natural law (in the strict sense) is determined on the basis of the content of a given commandment, i.e., if it is conceptually necessary that the commandment be valid. The "conceptually necessary", in this context, means necessary for the attainment of the ultimate end (the beatific vision) and this can be said only of those commandments that express self-evident principles (such as the first and the second commandment). Only such commandments prescribe goodness that cannot be repudiated without also repudiating the ultimate end. Cf. (Möhle 2003, pp. 314–16).

divine dispensation.[7] Following his interpretation of the Scriptures, Scotus identifies two purposes of marriage: the primary being procreation and the education of children, and the secondary being the avoidance of immorality. Furthermore, the principle underlying both of these purposes is the principle of justice.

Scotus was well aware that certain Old Testament patriarchs had more than one wife and, hence, he needed to provide an explanation as to whether they were given a divine dispensation as they practiced polygamy, and if so, what happened with the precept of natural law in such instances. His explanation builds on the notion of commutative justice, that for some, he argues, "requires quantitative equality not only proportional equity" (Wolter and Frank 1997, p. 185; *Ordinatio* b. IV, dist. 46). If this is true, he proceeds, then there is some imbalance in every marriage since "the male body is of more value than the female, for the same man could fecundate several women during the time it takes for the same woman to conceive through men" (Wolter and Frank 1997, p. 209; *Ordinatio* b.IV, dist. 33, q. 1). Consequently, if one judged marriage only on the basis of its primary purpose, there would be no reason to hold bigamy immoral. As opposed to this, when it comes to the secondary purpose of marriage (avoidance of immorality, i.e., fornication), male and female bodies are of equal value and, therefore, demand "one-to-one exchange of bodies" in order to satisfy justice.

This would seem to put the two purposes of marriage in opposition to each other and lead to the conclusion that since the primary purpose is, by definition, more important, it alone should be followed, even if the secondary one needs to be sacrificed. However, at this point Scotus introduces the will of the legislator (in this case, God) and argues: "Although some things belong to their owners, still what determines whether such and such an exchange is licit depends on the legislator, and this is true even more so as regards the mutual bodily exchange in the presence of a legislator who is God" (Wolter and Frank 1997, p. 209; *Ordinatio* b. IV, dist. 33, q. 1). Since, he continues, God has decreed that marriage should be between one man and one woman (the sixth commandment), what is just when it comes to marriage is clear.

Despite recognising the will of the legislator, Scotus does not deny the previous conclusion that on the basis of the primary purpose of marriage, bigamy is as reasonably acceptable as monogamy, if not more so. However, since the divine will has decreed otherwise in this case, it is impossible to make the case for the morality of bigamy without introducing the concept of divine dispensation, understood as revocation of the relevant precept in a particular case, and this is precisely what happened in the case of the Old Testament patriarchs. Namely, as Scotus explains, this happened in a situation in which the number of those who worship God was fairly small, and in order to increase their number, patriarchs were given a divine dispensation to marry more than one woman.

Interestingly, Scotus is not content with simply pointing towards the divine will that makes arbitrary decisions when it comes to the precepts of natural law in the extended sense (or precepts of divine positive law). In other words, it is not enough for him to point simply towards the divine will when answering the question why God decreed one way instead of the other when both options seem reasonable and possible. This is noticeable already in the fact that he provides a reason why God would give such a dispensation to the Old Testament patriarchs at all and, more importantly, he engages in a longer explanation in order to show the rational underpinnings of this divine intervention. Namely, he claims that "when there are two reasons why something is ordered, one the principal purpose, the (Wolter and Frank 1997, p. 210; *Ordinatio* b. IV, dist. 33, q. 1)[8]. Hence, one might imagine a situation

---

[7] Since the issue of marriage and bigamy is related to the sixth commandment (the second tablet), it is obvious that it does not concern the natural law in the strict sense or goodness that is necessarily linked to the attainment of the ultimate end.

[8] One of the anonymous reviewers of this article has argued that Scotus' way of reasoning through the problem of the relationship between marriage and bigamy does not seem to provide a convincing solution, since it seems to suggest that the only way of achieving one purpose of marriage is to go directly against the other, which would then make the natural law seem arbitrary. I believe that this critique stands only if the natural teloi of marriage are understood as principles that need to be followed or accommodated in any morally acceptable solution. As far as I understood Scotus, the two purposes of marriage should rather be understood as inconclusive indications of what would be a rational thing to do in this area of

where a war or an illness were to decimate the human population to such an extent that giving priority to the primary purpose of marriage would become just on the part of the contract and contracting parties; although, Scotus points out, "the complete justice" would still demand some kind of divine dispensation. Furthermore, Scotus does not exclude the possibility that such might be the case in the future and he even envisions that in such a situation divine dispensation could "then occur and be revealed in a special way to the Church" (Wolter and Frank 1997, p. 210; *Ordinatio* b. IV, dist. 33, q. 1)[9].

Related to this, Scotus rejects the "exception" explanation of divine dispensations by pointing to the principles of non-contradiction and internal coherence.[10] An added effect of these principles on Scotus' ethical theory in general and his treatment of divine dispensations in particular is that they allow, as we saw in the case of bigamy, a certain weighting of goods, depending on circumstances in which a precept or a commandment is to be applied. In other words, Scotus is not content with saying that a divine dispensation simply occurred in some instances, but aims at an explanation of why it occurred and this explanation reveals a rational procedure underlying a divine dispensation.

Further Issues

There are two issues that emerge in relation to this example. The first has to do with Scotus' attempt to find a balance between what is just according to reason and what is just according to the revealed divine will. Now these two coincide in Scotus' example to such an extent that he is fully justified in claiming that "where creatures are concerned he [God] is debtor rather to his generosity, in the sense that he gives creatures what their nature demands" (Wolter and Frank 1997, p. 190; *Ordinatio* b. IV, dist. 46). However, suppose that in some hypothetical case in the future (due to a nuclear war or a globally devastating disease) humankind were to diminish in number to such an extent that bigamy becomes simply necessary for the human species to survive. This would then satisfy Scotus' condition under which the primary purpose of marriage should be given the upper hand in determining what is the just (and, therefore, moral) thing to do, not to mention that the survival of the human species would depend on timely recognition of the special circumstances. Now, while Scotus would confirm that giving priority to the primary purpose of marriage in such circumstances is a just thing to do, he still demands divine dispensation in each particular case as a necessary requirement

---

life (and this is because there is no necessary relation between natural teloi and the ultimate end of human life for Scotus). They are inconclusive indications because the most Scotus can say is that there are rationally sound reasons to pursue only the primary purpose of marriage, as well as to pursue both primary and secondary purpose (although the latter solution already militates against the primary end to an extent, since one is not going to have as many children as one could by pursuing only the primary purpose of marriage). In order to turn these inconclusive indications into a rationally compelling argument (in the sense of recta ratio), circumstances need to be considered (and the argument needs to be sanctioned by the divine will). Nevertheless, since these inconclusive indications are both rationally sound, none of the possible solutions would make natural laws related to them internally incoherent (in the sense of irrational or incomprehensible).

9   This is exactly opposite of the claim made by Ansgar Santogrossi who tried to summarise Scotus' position on dispensations by formulating a contemporary Scotistic gloss: "A contemporary Scotistic gloss on the pope's [John Paul II] words might run: given the categorical, universal character of St. Paul's condemnation of certain acts falling under the second table of the Decalogue, the closure of revelation with the death of the last apostle, and the obvious thrust of the *Veritatis splendor*, it can be stated that it will never be licit to act against the divine precept 'till heaven and earth pass away', regardless of how the Old Testament loci for dispensations from those precepts should be interpreted; nevertheless in the last analysis this is because God has graciously and contingently willed it so" (Santogrossi 1994, p. 326). Although I can agree with Santogrossi that, according to Scotus, God's gracious and contingent decision of the will is certainly responsible for the OT dispensations, Scotus is quite clear that such dispensations both occurred and can still occur. Hence, Santogrossi's limitation of the scope of the divine contingent will, introduced in order to bring it in line with *Veritatis splendor*, is clearly misplaced. Apart from that, if the possibility of dispensing from precepts of natural law in the extended sense is a prerogative of God's gracious and contingent will, then denying this prerogative is an expression of hubris that reserves for itself another prerogative of knowing better how God's graciousness should be exercised and, naturally, it should never be exercised in opposition to what is expected of it.

10 The reason why Scotus rejects the "exception" explanation of divine dispensation, as Möhle explains, consists in the fact that he holds the principles of non-contradiction and coherence as valid, even when it comes to what God can do, due to his absolute power. From these two, Scotus argues that God cannot order the world in such a way that the precepts of that ordering would contradict each other. Even more, these precepts have to constitute a coherent whole. Hence, if the "exception" explanation of divine dispensations were to be valid, then God could simply disregard these two principles, while decisions of his will would have an arbitrary character. Cf. (Möhle 2003, p. 321).

for what he calls "complete justice". But, suppose that human species or, at least, the community of believers does not receive such dispensation, because, as Scotus himself claims, "in truth nothing outside of God can be said to be definitely just [... ;] where a creature is concerned, God is just only in relationship to his first justice, namely, because such a creature has been actually willed by the divine will" (Wolter and Frank 1997, p. 190; *Ordinatio* b. IV, dist. 46).

In my opinion, this passage and Scotus' insistence on the freedom of the divine will argues in favour of the possibility that in the above hypothetical case, the human species might not receive the needed divine dispensation or, in a milder form of the argument, it might not recognise it. If this is possible, then one would have to conclude that, in the first case (of not receiving divine dispensation), what is just according to reason, namely, preservation of the human species, is at the same time unjust according to the divine will and vice versa. In other words, one would have to conclude that in the perspective of "complete justice" it is morally wrong for the human species to do what they deem necessary and reasonable for their own preservation in the given circumstances, which seems counterintuitive.

On the other hand, the second case (of not recognising divine dispensation) raises a different issue of the form in which the divine dispensation should appear. Building on the Old Testament cases of divine dispensations, Scotus somewhat predisposes us to think of some kind of supernatural intervention, but should this necessarily be so? Is it not also imaginable to think of divine dispensation becoming manifest through dictates of right reason, especially in such an extreme case? Of course, this would also mean that in such a situation ethicists could not aim for certain knowledge, since, according to Scotus, one is not dealing here with necessary truths, but with contingent ones that depend on decisions of the divine will. However, if this is the case, then a divine dispensation would only confirm the insight gained through reason and, therefore, make it certain, but the issue remains whether such certainty is absolutely necessary for moral decision making and moral action. A renowned Scotistic scholar, Allan Wolter, would agree with this and argue in favour of the quasi-sufficiency of right reason:

> Even the sort of dispensations Scotus sees God making [...] are always in accord with right reason, and are something the human mind did figure out, or might have if emotions did not blind one's reason. For they concern such things as are good for man [sic] in relation to his fellowman, where there is a hierarchy of values involved, and where to obtain the principal value, certain aspects of lesser value may have to be sacrificed, in view of a less than ideal environmental situation. (Wolter and Frank 1997, pp. 26–27)

The second issue related to the above example points towards the not-so-hypothetical case of over-population on the planet or in some regions in the world. If one were to continue to follow the same logic as I used in my analysis of the previous issue, then one would have to conclude that this drastic change in circumstances should also reflect on how one applies Scotus' purposes of marriage. In other words, if the secondary purpose of marriage has to be sacrificed in a situation where the survival of the species might well depend on giving priority to the primary purpose of marriage, should the reverse not also hold when the population has increased to such an extent that its numbers threaten its own survival and make the possibility of a total war for the world's resources quite imaginable? Of course, apart from giving some kind of priority to the secondary purpose of marriage (avoidance of fornication or, more positively, companionship or love), this argument does not resolve entirely what God's will in such a case might be (celibacy? natural family planning? contraception?), but it certainly shows the direction in which *recta ratio*, at least as envisioned by Scotus, would point (Wolter and Frank 1997, p. 72).[11] Furthermore, these two extreme cases of underpopulation and overpopulation suggest that Scotus is content with postulating the existence of only one absolute

---

[11] In these issues related to the example of bigamy, I followed Scotus' distinction between primary and secondary purpose of marriage in order to see where his reasoning would take us when it comes to various situations and to demonstrate

value, God himself and how we relate to him, while being aware that human values (and how they are realised in concrete norms, behaviour, and acts) do not (and does not) suffer absolute and universal solutions, unless one is willing to sacrifice *recta ratio*.

Being true to the *recta ratio*, on the other hand, demands bringing together the first principle of praxis, the conclusions of moral science, and the specific conditions under which the act is considered. Apart from the first principle of praxis that already grounds reasons' deliberations in objective reality, the notions of "seeing" and "hearing" that Scotus uses in this context, also hint at something objective that is present and that needs to be recognised and taken into consideration by the agent (Ingham and Dreyer 2004, pp. 176–77). These, of course, refer to goods that are a part of objective reality and dividable into useful goods (*bonum utile*) and goods of value (*bonum honestum*) that correspond to the affection for the advantageous and the affection for justice, respectively. Starting from these, rational judgment will also have to take into consideration other conditions (such as, whether the act is done for right reason, at the right time and place, in the right manner, and as a prudential person would perform it) in order to satisfy the demand for objectivity. It is clear from this that Scotus' insistence on the primacy of *recta ratio* is not a flight into moral subjectivism, but an affirmation of the nature of moral reasoning that presupposes and takes into consideration objective reality (both necessary and contingent), while at the same time it escapes the naïve approach of reducing moral deliberations to deductive reasoning and instead likens it to aesthetic judgments.

5. Conclusions

Although a more detailed argument in favour of recruiting Scotus as a source for reframing Catholic theological ethics would demand an overview of his whole ethical theory, as well as an engagement with its finer details, even this short paper based on a particular issue he dealt with allows one to draw out some preliminary conclusions. In what follows, these preliminary conclusions will be presented in terms of the previously mentioned methodological points of convergence between Scotus and Selling: (1) the notion of premoral and moral good and evil, (2) the primary importance of the end in the specification and evaluation of moral acts, and (3) the (ir)relevancy of the concept of intrinsic evil.[12]

5.1. The Notion of Premoral and Moral Good and Evil

In order to make his argument that the presence of evil or a disvalue in a human act does not necessarily mean that the act is morally evil, Selling uses the distinction between premoral and moral good/evil and relates the former to Aquinas' notion of natural good/evil and the manualist notion of physical evil (Selling 2016, pp. 171–86).[13] However, the counter-argument in this sense (for instance, from the proponents of the New Natural Law Theory) claims that one should never act directly against a basic good (Finnis 2011, pp. 118–24), and one of the reasons, I suspect, that lies behind the coherence of this claim is the previously mentioned close connection between the precepts of the law of nature and the order of natural inclinations that Aquinas posited.

---

that there is an underlying method to his reasoning. Of course, if we were to apply his method to contemporary Catholic teaching on marriage (that does not distinguish between primary and secondary ends of marriage, although it claims that the ends of marriage are inseparable), the results would be different.

12 In formulating these three points of convergence I am indebted to Thomas Shannon. Cf. (Shannon 1995, pp. 87–113).
13 By premoral evil Selling refers to those realities, specified descriptively, that are harmful to human beings (hence, –moral), but are not immediately morally determinative (hence, pre-), such as death, sickness, ignorance, etc. Similarly, premoral goods are those realities that are beneficial to human beings, but are not immediately morally determinative, such as health, nutrition, knowledge, etc. The notion of moral good/evil, on the other hand, always implies a reference to the human will intending how to bring about a certain end and choosing means to it. In this sense, Selling would argue that sometimes one can choose a premoral evil as a means of attaining a good end (for instance, punishing a criminal to attain justice in a society) and this kind of premoral evil does not make the whole act morally evil. However, he warns, "the manner or extent to which some evil may be attached to the moral event [...] is not always straightforward". (Selling 2016, p. 181).

I believe that this is a point where Scotus' approach can be of some use. Namely, the problem with erasing or disregarding the distinction between premoral and moral goods/evils in writings of some contemporary moral theologians is that (at least some) goods assume an almost absolute character. On the other hand, Scotus acknowledges the importance of the precepts of the second tablet of the Decalogue, since they are in harmony with the natural law in the strict sense and a part of the moral order that God established for this world, but refuses, as we saw in the example of marriage and bigamy, to treat them in an absolute way by proposing a universal, one-size-fits-all, short-circuited solution to ethical dilemmas, wherever these "absolute" values appear. This does not only mean that theoretically and metaphysically the moral order could have been different, it also means that his understanding of goods and how they constitute moral goods is more dynamic, since, as he claims: "The precepts of the second table contain no goodness such as is necessarily prescribed for attaining the goodness of the ultimate end, nor in what is forbidden is there such malice as would turn one away necessarily from the last end" (Wolter and Frank 1997, p. 277; *Ordinatio* b. 3, dist. 27). Apart from the implications that this position has for the role of *recta ratio* in moral reasoning, one could also argue that it is compatible with the distinction between premoral and moral goods, as well as with the human person being the standard for theological ethics, as Selling suggests (Selling 2016, chp. 5).

5.2. The Primary Importance of the End in the Specification and Evaluation of Moral Acts

Because of the later emphasis on the object of the act during the manualist period, Selling dedicates a good portion of his book to demonstrating the primary importance of the end in the specification and evaluation of human acts in Aquinas' *Treatise on Human Acts* (Selling 2016, pp. 62–82). This, again, is a contested point in contemporary theological ethics that often leads to endless discussions on how Aquinas should be interpreted. There is much less controversy, on the other hand, related to Scotus' treatment of this topic. First of all, Aquinas, Scotus, and Selling agree on the claim that the end takes precedence in the specification and evaluation of human acts, but Aquinas' explanation of the relation between the end and the object is convoluted and leaves room for contrary interpretations, as evidenced by the whole manualist tradition and the post-conciliar debates within the field of theological ethics.

Scotus' approach, on the other hand, is simpler, but perhaps more elegant. He first claims that the goodness of an act depends on whether it possesses "all that the agent's right reason declares must pertain to the act or the agent in acting" (Alluntis and Wolter 1975, p. 400; Quodlibet q. 18, a. 1) and the right reason judges this from the nature of the terms or from intellectual knowledge. Put differently, if one knows the nature of the agent, the power by which the agent acts, and has the essential notion of the act one is equipped to judge the appropriateness of particular acts. According to Scotus, this is done by first identifying the object of an act, which is identified with 'matter' (such as food being the object of the act of eating) or 'moral matter' (such as taking what belongs to another being the object of the act of theft). However, the object merely puts the act in the moral domain and opens it to further moral determination, which is done by considering the circumstances of the act. The most important and morally determinative circumstance is the end and, therefore, the most one could say about an act on the basis of the object alone is that it tends towards good or evil, but it is, strictly speaking, morally indifferent. Scotus clearly demonstrates this approach in his treatment of marriage and bigamy in which the importance of shifting circumstances and especially the end plays a determinative role in the ethical evaluation of the whole issue and the acts associated with it.[14] As such, it ought to be

---

[14] The end as a circumstance is the end of an agent, which could be any of the two goods associated (for Scotus) with marriage or both. His point (and mine in presenting and developing his point) is that one cannot exclude a priori any of these two (or three) possibilities as being always immoral, since circumstances might demand giving priority to one of the goods associated with marriage (provided a divine dispensation has also been given). Since these goods are both relative in relation to the ultimate end, they do not always have to be pursued by the will when one intends marriage (such as in the case of underpopulation (Scotus) or overpopulation (my deduction)).

5.3. The (Ir)Relevancy of the Concept of Intrinsic Evil

At various points in his study, Selling argues that the notion of intrinsic evil ought to be eliminated from Catholic ethical discourse, since, as a product of an inaccurate manualist reading of Aquinas, it does not contribute anything to ethical discernment and is simply confusing as it generally leaves the impression that acts can be morally evaluated on the basis of an inadequate description (Selling 2016, pp. 162, 179, 200). Although this is contrary to Aquinas' way of thinking in *Summa Theologiae* I-II, there are still some places where he leaves the impression that some objects (i.e., what is done) can never be a part of a morally good act—such as in *De malo*, q. 2, aa. 3-4 and in *Summa Theologiae* I-II, q. 20. a. 2.

On the other hand, Scotus is quite clear on this point by allowing only one absolute intrinsic value, and that is God himself.[15] Consequently, there is only one object that can never be a part of a morally good act, and that is hatred of God. Since the obligation to worship God is part of the natural law in the strict sense that expresses a necessary truth, not even God can make such knowledge false or give a dispensation from this obligation.

In that sense all other values are relative. In other words, they are a part of this current moral order, in harmony with the natural law in the strict sense, and, as such, willed by God for our good and conducive to our salvation. However, Scotus claims that it is possible "for me to will that my neighbour love God and nevertheless not will that he preserves corporeal life or conjugal fidelity" (Wolter and Frank 1997, p. 285; *Ordinatio* b. III, dist. 27), while his treatment of marriage and bigamy, as well as the other Old Testament dispensations, illustrates this point as a "fact", i.e., as (moral) events that took place.

5.4. Scotus' Contemporary Significance

One of the main achievements of Selling's book *Reframing Catholic Theological Ethics* is that it appeals to a reader's ethical imagination by posing the question—what is it that we are trying to achieve in our moral lives in the first place? Seen from this perspective, the manual tradition's focus on acts, objects, and moral pathology (sins) is revealed as one possible answer to this question within the Catholic tradition and not the Tradition itself. Selling suggests further that returning to Aquinas' text in *Summa theologiae* offers another possible answer and an exploration of Scotus' thought, attempted in this article, promises yet another answer within that same tradition.

Despite a contrary judgement found within the more recent history of the discipline of theological ethics that dismissed Scotus' ethical thought as highly suspicious in terms of its compatibility with the Catholic tradition, contemporary engagement with his thought demonstrated that Scotus is closer to Aquinas on some key points than Aquinas' later commentators (Salzman 1995, pp. 375–88). This is certainly true when it comes to what was later called *fontes moralitatis* (object, end, and circumstances) and the insistence of both Scotus and Aquinas that the end takes precedence in the specification of human acts. From this point, as the article showed, Scotus develops his thought in a different direction than Aquinas. However, an urgent task of rethinking the ends of our ethical striving within

---

[15] By using a case study of lying Richard Cross has argued that Scotus is in fact a proponent of the concept of intrinsically evil acts as those acts that are morally wrong on the basis of their object. According to Cross, Scotus' list of such acts would not include only hatred of God, but also lying, murder, theft, and adultery. It is impossible to evaluate Cross' carefully argued claims within the frame of this article, since one would first have to discuss how Scotus and then Cross understand objects of the abovementioned acts and only then proceed to engage with the claims Cross has made. Another problem with the case study of lying is that Scotus seemed to have stopped somewhere in the middle between, on the one hand, what he encountered in the tradition (especially Augustinian tradition) and other medieval theologians when it comes to lying and, on the other hand, bringing his reflection on lying more in line with the more general direction of his own thought that goes beyond the natural teleology approach. This is what makes Cross' claim debatable and Scotus' treatment of lying as, perhaps, not the most representative of his thought. Cf. (Cross 1997, pp. 48–76).

contemporary theological ethics and letting go of the fascination with moral pathology, encounters in Scotus a challenging dialogical partner whose ideas can significantly expand the horizon of the discipline while keeping it firmly grounded in the tradition.

Conflicts of Interest: The author declares no conflict of interest. The founding sponsors had no role in the design of the study; in the collection, analyses, or interpretation of data; in the writing of the manuscript, and in the decision to publish the results.

References

Alluntis, Felix, and Allan B. Wolter. 1975. *John Duns Scotus: God and Creatures: The Quodlibetal Questions.* Washington: The Catholic University of America Press.

Aquinas, Thomas. 1955–1957. Summa contra gentiles. Available online: http://dhspriory.org/thomas/ContraGentiles.htm (accessed on 26 April 2017).

Cross, Richard. 1997. Duns Scotus on Goodness, Justice, and what God Can Do. *Journal of Theological Studies* 48: 48–76. [CrossRef]

Finnis, John. 2011. *Natural Law and Natural Rights.* Oxford: Oxford University Press.

Ingham, Mary B., and Mechthild Dreyer. 2004. *The Philosophical Vision of John Duns Scotus: An Introduction.* Washington: Catholic University of America Press.

Jaczn, Antoon V., Henri Veldhuis, Aline H. Looman-Graaskamp, Eef Dekker, and Nico W. den Bok. 1994. *John Duns Scotus: Contingency and Freedom: Lectura I 39.* Dordrecht: Kluwer Academic Publishers.

Leo, XIII. 1879. Aeterni Patris. Available online: http://w2.vatican.va/content/leo-xiii/en/encyclicals/documents/hf_l-xiii_enc_04081879_aeterni-patris.html (accessed on 26 April 2017).

McCormick, Richard A. 1981. *Notes on Moral Theology 1965–1980.* Washington: University Press of America.

Möhle, Hannes. 2003. Scotus's Theory of Natural Law. In *The Cambridge Companion to Duns Scotus.* Edited by Thomas Williams. Cambridge: Cambridge University Press, pp. 312–31.

Osborne, Thomas M. 2014. *Human Action in Thomas Aquinas, John Duns Scotus & William of Ockham.* Washington: Catholic University of America Press.

Pickstock, Catherine. 2005. Duns Scotus: His Historical and Contemporary Significance. *Modern Theology* 21: 543–74. [CrossRef]

Salzman, Todd. 1995. *Deontology and Teleology: An Investigation of the Normative Debate in Roman Catholic Moral Theology.* Leuven: Leuven University Press.

Santogrossi, Ansgar. 1994. Scotus's Method in Ethics: Not to Play God—A Reply to Thomas Shannon. *Theological Studies* 55: 314–29. [CrossRef]

Selling, Joseph A. 2016. *Reframing Catholic Theological Ethics.* Oxford: Oxford University Press.

Shannon, Thomas A. 1995. *The Ethical Theory of John Duns Scotus.* Quincy: Franciscan Press.

Wolter, Allan B., and William A. Frank. 1997. *Duns Scotus on the Will and Morality.* Washington: The Catholic University of America Press.

© 2017 by the author. Licensee MDPI, Basel, Switzerland. This article is an open access article distributed under the terms and conditions of the Creative Commons Attribution (CC BY) license (http://creativecommons.org/licenses/by/4.0/).

Article

Hermeneutic and Teleology in Ethics across Denominations—Thomas Aquinas and Karl Barth

Jacqueline Stewart

Department of Theology and Religion, University of Exeter, Exeter EX4, UK; jacqueline.stewart@exeter.ac.uk[1]

Received: 17 August 2017; Accepted: 17 September 2017; Published: 27 September 2017

Abstract: This study arises from the context of current debates in the Catholic Church on the place of rule and law in moral reasoning. I suggest that ethics may be best served by approaches that place the human subject in a teleogical context and that recognise the need for interpretation of circumstances surrounding actions to be evaluated. This is in contrast to normative rule approaches. The insights retrieved from the account of moral reasoning in Thomas Aquinas by Joseph Selling are compared with an account of the ethical implications of Karl Barth's theology of hope as expressed in Volume Four of the *Church Dogmatics*. It is concluded that, in an ecumenical convergence, neither propose a normative rule approach. Rather both use a teleological context and require a hermeneutic of evaluation.

Keywords: moral theology; ethics; hermeneutics; discernment; moral development; intention; Thomas Aquinas; Karl Barth

1. Introduction

A contemporary 'reframing' may be indicated for moral theology and ethics across the whole range of denominations and even religions. There are historical factors in play including changes in social, economic and political spheres in Western Europe. The first half of the twentieth century, marked by two world wars, was nevertheless a period of general social conformity, with widely accepted social values on matters such as sexual behaviour, citizenship, social and political institutions. After the end of the Second World War, the so called 'post war consensus' was increasingly disturbed and in the succeeding fifty years, broken up entirely. Changes in the role of women and the family, enabled by the advent of safe contraception, challenges to economic theory and distrust of the role of authority after the excesses of the war, were associated with an increasing individualism, and desire for personal freedom. More extreme political positions emerged, including the rise of right wing politics which looked back to the emotional security of the pre-war certainties. The shrinking of the effect and influence of social institutions was accompanied by increasing secularisation. The churches lost members and influence, and their right to a voice in public discourse became more precarious. Calum Brown's study on the decline of church influence, particularly the last chapter, (Brown 2001) and Tony Judt's contribution on economic changes (Judt 2010) are among many which provide insights into some of these changes.

These trends were paralleled by change within the churches. In the Catholic Church, the Second Vatican Council allowed the dissatisfaction with the imposed conformity of the preceding era to be expressed. It matched the ferment and flowering of ideas that was being expressed in secular society. In the following decades, it was succeeded by increasing concern about secularisation and the loss of church influence. Matching the rise of ultra conservative politics outside, currents in the Church

---

[1] The author is also an Honorary Senior Lecturer in Theology at the University of Leeds, Leeds LS2 9JT, UK.

favoured a return to conformist values and practice. Church members valued certainty and wanted moral guidance in a pluralist and chaotic world.

This is part of the background to the contemporary debates in moral theology and ethics. In the Catholic Church, there is a significant debate about the status of moral laws and rules, with a spectrum of views. At one end, there are those influenced by the reforms of Vatican II, who regard moral laws and rules as necessary but not sufficient, potentially ambiguous and therefore neither normative nor certain in all situations. At the other end, there are those who are concerned by the loss of the Church's role in society since Vatican II, and who regard moral law as primary, unambiguous, normative for all action and certain as a guide to right action. This debate obtains in Protestant theologies as well as in Roman Catholic ones. It has practical consequences in that, on one hand, the existence of normative rules supports cohesion within groups, and strengthens their identity in the face of unwanted outside influence. On the other hand, an interpretative approach to ethical decision making allows for pastoral sensitivity, and is flexible when encountering new problems.

In the Roman Catholic Church, an actual controversy has developed between those at each end of this spectrum. For instance, the encylical *Veritatis Splendor* promoted a narrow reading of natural law and stressed a revisionist evaluation of action against rule or law. More recently, those following the more expansive ideas expressed in Vatican II have been given more of a hearing. In preparation for the consultation of bishops by Pope Francis at the 2014 Synod on the Family, Bishop Bonny of Antwerp noted that after the publication of the encyclical *Humanae Vitae*, official Church teaching was often identified with a version of the normative rule approach. At the same time, representatives of other approaches were, he said, "consigned to the corner as suspicious and to be avoided." They included "highly meritorious theologians . . . Josef Fuchs SJ, Bernard Häring CSsR and L. Janssens (KU Leuven)". He observed that "different moral-theological models have always functioned within the church", and he cites the encyclical *Evangelii Gaudium* in support of the importance of diverse traditions and argumentation in the pursuit of truth. (Bonny 2014, pp. 9–10). These ideas of moral hermeneutic have been rehabilitated in *Amoris Laetitia*, notably in Chapter 8, where Pope Francis comments on the need for discernment of situations, and this is discussed elsewhere in this journal.

2. 'End' to 'Intention' to 'Act'; Teleological Priority and Hermeneutic Necessity in Thomas

Against the foregoing background, the contributions of Joe Selling to the Catholic tradition can be seen to be very important He studied with Louis Janssens (Janssens 1988) and has expanded and developed the insights that Janssens brought to moral theology (Selling 2016). These emerged from the re-reading of Thomas that took place before Vatican II, in which the foundational theological intentions of Thomas were re explored. In a major insight, Janssens expounded the distinction Thomas makes between intention, and choice, and the prior moral significance he imputes to intention. Janssens develops this to the conclusion that Thomas does not offer a rule based normativity. Rather, he proposes a process of moral reasoning requiring an interpretation of tradition in which humanity is oriented to the pursuit of the good, and which sees the moral importance of intention, and takes into account the finite and partial nature of human reality. (From this account of moral reasoning in Thomas, the description of moral action as involving the 'human person adequately considered' evolved and found its way into the documents of Vatican II). This also restores the universality of Thomas' position, since orientation to ultimate good and intent to do good in pursuit of that is not restricted to Christians. It seems to me that the key points in Selling's reading of Thomas are firstly, his attention to the structure of the *Summa Theologiae* as Thomas intended it. Selling points out that Thomas adapted the conventional pattern of medieval theological treatises in his grouping of material. In Part I, Thomas deals first with the actions of God, and then with humanity as created. The implications of this are made clear; the telos of humanity is that it should ultimately flourish with God at the End. By virtue of being created by God, humanity is called or oriented to the good. Thomas is interested in voluntary acts, that is, those resulting from the operation of the will, because only those are subject to moral evaluation. His understanding of will is that it is the "intellectual appetite, whereby the person is attracted towards that which is apprehended as true and good" (Selling 2016, p. 59). His reading of the human being parallels Aristotle; nobody does things that they think are bad for themselves at a foundational level. That is, what is desirable presents as what is good. The ideas that people have about what is good may be perverted, but the foundational orientation of the human is to what is perceived as good. (Selling 2016, pp. 59–60). Thomas describes human beings as characterised by capacity, capability or agency. Only in Part II Section 1 of the Summa does Thomas come to the specifics of the capacity for moral reasoning and behaviour, and in Part II.2 to the dispositions helpful to developing it. Selling demonstrates convincingly that Thomas sees moral or ethical behaviour as resulting from a process, (which Selling terms 'the moral event') originating in the divinely created human capacity for orientation to the good. Thomas begins with the evaluation of the end or goal of action. Thomas says "the end is last in execution, but first in intention of reason, according to which moral actions receive their species" (Selling 2016, p. 62). Selling contends that Thomas then works through the components of a 'moral event' from the overall goal through intention and aspects of context to the concrete behaviour. Selling summarises this in his schema, which is discussed elsewhere in this journal,

"End > intention > circumstances > behaviour > act/object " (Selling 2016, p. 170)

In this account of moral decision making and reasoning, the human *telos*, the orientation to God as ultimate, drives intention which requires interpretation of circumstances, hermeneutics, to formulate behaviour. Selling argues that while Thomas was concerned with the basic ethical commitment of a person, those who came after him were more interested in specific behaviours. Consequently, generations missed the significance and value of his discussion, and focused on objectified virtues and vices instead. This oversight may have contributed to the predominance of rule based thinking in the moral theology of the eighteenth and nineteenth century manuals. Daniel Westberg offers an approach to Thomas which converges with Selling, (Westberg 2015), in distinction to the many who would maintain a contrary view, e.g., Sevais Pinckaers (Pinckaers 2001).

It seems that Selling's recovery of insights from Thomas, via the approaches that were present in Vatican II, may alter the balance of argument between those advocating normative rules and those advocating an interpretative context in the Roman Catholic tradition. What of Protestant approaches to moral and ethical thinking? Karl Barth is often described as one of the most significant Protestant theologians of the twentieth century (Webster 2000). His approach to moral reasoning may yield some valuable insights in the context of the foregoing discussion.

3. Barth and Contemporary Protestant Ethics

There is a vast literature on Barth's ethics. Work in English can be divided rather arbitrarily into three phases. There was an early phase in the 1970s, when some authors began to explore some the radical implications of Barth's theology—for example, the notable Gifford lectures by Stanley Hauerwas (Hauerwas 2001). Then there was a phase in the 1990s when authors such a Nigel Biggar re-examined the ethical dimension of Barth's foundational theology (Biggar 1993). And most recently, in the last decade and a half, there has been a turn to so called 'Protestant Thomism', which often draws on Barth for support. Recent work includes the compilation of essays in *Commanding Grace* (Migliore 2010), *Behaving in Public* (Biggar 2011), *Aquinas as Authority* (Van Geest et al. 2002) and articles such as 'Practical Wisdom and the Integrity of Christian Life' (Werpehowski 2007). The whole issue of *Studies in Christian Ethics* in 2013 was devoted to this area. The major part of all this work has mostly been associated with attempts to recover an approach to natural law consonant with contemporary protestant sensibilities, as part of an attempt to create an ethical discourse that can meet secular debate in the public arena on common ground. This is likely to prove a hard row to hoe, not least because Barth himself specifically objected to rule based ethics, and objected very definitely indeed to arguments from natural law. His objections stem from his foundational concern to allow God to speak from scripture and tradition, rather than allowing human projections onto scripture and tradition to create idolatrous versions of God. Barth did not ignore the questions about how people can act rightly, but he had very different answers from his contemporaries. Webster encapsulates Barth's view when he says "Barth takes a radically different approach: describing the moral field is not a matter of analysing judgements made, but of portraying the encounter of God with humanity with as much density as possible" (Webster 1995, p. 100).

Before Barth's approach to ethics can be set out, it is essential to explore the issue of his use of language. A proper understanding of Barth, like Thomas, requires that parts are read in the light of the whole. Barth uses the language of "command", "summoning", "response" etc. in the context of human response to the "Word". To make sense of this, it is helpful to know that every significant word in Barth is written in the context of the direct relation of God and humanity. As used by Barth, these words can be only be properly understood when redefined in the light of the Christ event. The commands that Jesus gives and himself responds to are the imperatives of love, and this is what Barth intends. For example, obedience in Barth means a loving response to the call of Christ, not a submission to some kind of objectified power. George Hunsinger has an excellent account of this and other issues raised by Barth's creative use of language (Hunsinger 1991, p. 33ff). Consequently, it is possible to respectfully disagree with, for instance, Nigel Biggar's approach to translating "command" in which he fits various humanly constructed meanings (the military, the legal) to Barth's use of the word (Biggar 2010, pp. 28–31). It may be thought that this misses the fundamental ethical implications of the word as Barth uses it. Given Barth's view of human situatedness, it is not surprising that he sees ethical behaviour and moral action as responsive behaviour and action. It follows that when Nimmo discusses Barth's view of the human being as a moral agent, he asserts that "to answer the ethical question of what it means to be a responsible Christian . . . we are directed to Jesus Christ . . . we are summoned by this Word of God to obedient action in freedom and love" (Nimmo 2010, p. 232). Here again 'responsible' means responsive in and to love; 'summoned' means lovingly called into love, 'obedient' means freely consenting to love. The invitation to relationship given by the sense of 'God with us' is not an "arbitrary act of the divine omnipotence of grace" (Barth 1956–1975, vol. IV/I, p. 12); it is not being overridden by an impersonal goodness. Rather it is the most loving personal outreach, where God himself involved himself as God and man in "a real closing of the breach, gulf and abyss" (Barth 1956–1975, vol. IV/I, p. 12) between God and humans. The problem is the belief of the human "that he can and should find self-fulfillment. He has himself become an eschaton" (Barth 1956–1975, vol. IV/I, p. 10); that is, humans attempt to become their own end and goal, thus perverting their proper destiny. Rather than this refusal of relation, which constitutes sin, Barth is clear that love is foundational to the Christian response to this call to relationship. Thomas would surely agree with this.

The overall sweep of Barth's thought is set out in his monumental work on theology, *Church Dogmatics* (Barth 1956–1975), which is structured in four developing sections. Volume One, *The Doctrine of The Word*, is an account of the possibility of knowing God; Volume Two, *The Doctrine of God*, is an account of some of what may be known of God; Volume Three, *The Doctrine of Creation*, is an account of God's foundational activity in relation to humanity. Irrupting into this is the tragic fact of human sin and rejection of God. The story of God and humanity is completed by Barth with Volume Four, *The Doctrine of Reconciliation*, which includes a treatment of the virtues of faith, hope and charity. It should be noted that these works came to fruition through a time span of over twenty years. There are therefore changes in direction and emphasis as Barth's thinking developed. There is no section in the *Church Dogmatics* headed 'ethics'. His explicit conclusions on ethical and moral reasoning are mostly found in Volume Four and they center on the practical implications of what faith, hope and charity might mean in the context of the human relation with Jesus Christ. One should bear in mind here John Webster's argument that the whole of the *Dogmatics* has a foundationally ethical character (Webster 1995, 1998).

An example of the working out of Barth's ethics can be found in his treatment of hope. Barth begins his survey of reconciliation with a summary of the core of the Christian message that Jesus Christ is the cosmic reconciler, and is the fundamental and foundational renewer of all reality (Barth 1956–1975, vol. IV/1, p. 3). Consequently, humanity has indeed certain hope in God, because nothing could be more certain and reliable than the faithfulness of God in Jesus Christ, and that hope is sustained and empowered by the Spirit. The formation of the Christian community follows the Spirit's empowerment of the human response to the invitation to hope in Christ. Barth notes the key features of such hope—empowered life, active engagement in community, and enervation by a non- simplistic vision of the Holy Spirit. All of these have ethical implications.

4. An Example: Barth on the Ethical Implications of Hope

Firstly—For Barth, hope is not about judgement and the last things. Hope is not hope *for* things but rather *in* Christ, in a person. Hope is explained in the context of community, the body of Christ in whom Christians hope, and it has ethical implications, as being in a relationship of hope and trust transforms the life of the Christian. It also stands clearly as distinct from human expectation or fate, the mechanical unfolding of determined events. That hope for Barth is both personal and relational hope in Jesus Christ, is further illustrated by John McDowell in his explorations of the Barth—Brunner controversy (McDowell 2006). Interestingly, McDowell cites the support of Rahner (1961–1992); "Christ himself is the hermeneutical principle of all eschatological assertions. Anything that cannot be read and understood as a christological assertion is not a genuine eschatological assertion" (McDowell 2006, p. 35). McDowell is clear that "for Barth, Christian hope is not an expectation of some external object or thing, nor a belief in an automatically unfolding future ordained by some *deus ex machina*". Similarly, Gerhard Sauter can argue, over against Moltmann (1967), that Barth's theology is not a kind of futurism or 'theology of hope' (Sauter 1999, p. 408).

Hope is what humans are summoned to, it is a calling from God into a relationship with Jesus Christ with all the consequences that entails, and this is surely compatible with Selling's reading of Thomas. The Christian does not project himself into the future by expectation or anticipation, which would be an unreliable proceeding depending on his own finite effort, but is called from the future by Jesus Christ as risen, vindicated Lord. Christian faith, love and hope are focused on the person who calls humanity into relation, Christ. Jesus Christ is both the hope of the Christian and that which makes such hope possible. Barth says of Christian hope that Jesus Christ is

> "...the theme and goal and basis of his subjective hope. Nor is it that he merely is his hope...Jesus Christ, who does not merely accompany and precede him in time, who also comes to meet him from its end and goal, makes possible his being as Christian and witness even in the apparently dark time and empty time which is before him, including the hour of death." (Barth 1956–1975, vol. IV/3.2, p. 915).

Here it is clear that hoping in Christ empowers 'being as Christian' and 'witness'; as Webster observes, it involves action, orientation, effectiveness in concrete human life (Webster 1998, pp. 95–96) In fact, hope is a calling to ethical behaviour.

Secondly—At the outset, it can be seen that Barth preserves the priority of God's reconciling activity in respect of human responses to it. Humanity is not saved because people have faith in a particular formula, or are baptised into a particular community, or follow particular practices (Barth 1956–1975, vol. IV/1, p. 4). The possibility of hope is a cosmic reality for all. Barth's account combines both the subjective availability of Jesus Christ as known in the Christian community and his objective reality as cosmic enabler of the hope that community has. Jesus Christ himself is the hope of both Christians and also non-Christians. The reality of hope does not depend on conscious knowledge of or about Christ. Barth observes "Whether known now or unknown, He is the future of all" (Barth 1956–1975, vol. IV/3.1, p. 346). Christian hope is not about securing a kind of salvation limited to the self, ('pie in the sky when you die'), but about the promise to all. Note that in Barth, being is always be-ing, an act of a dynamic subject, not a property of a static object. Hunsinger's discussion of actualism illuminates this (Hunsinger 1991). Similarly, for Barth, reconciliation is not a condition, but an ongoing event (Barth 1956–1975, vol. IV.1, pp. 3–6). For Barth, as for Thomas, humans are created, embedded in a relation of love, called and empowered to respond to God's love. And since responsive hope is in Christ, it is inevitably a calling or orientation to the ultimate good. Again, Selling's account of Thomas converges on this.

In conclusion, Barth argues that hope leads to concrete witness—a relation of trust in another person brings about change. It can give courage, it can lead to a desire to make a practical response, and it can strengthen shared values and uncover new ones. The responsibility for 'reading the signs of the times', for consideration and evaluation, lies with the human individual. Barth accepts that human intellectual assessment of concrete circumstances involves a process of interpretation, that is, a hermeneutic. Scripture and tradition provide guidance, but the Spirit-empowered person uses what is given in the relation with Christ to choose the best path. Such change also implies effort and struggle against evil and sin. Here again, the commitment to the good is prior and it informs intentions for actions, as in Selling's explication of Thomas. Barth's conception of Christian hope gives it ethical force; Christians are summoned to hope, and hope is participation in a relation with Jesus Christ. He himself, rather than a humanly constructed rule or law, is the practical standard of evaluation for the life that is conferred by the relationship with him. Christian hope is not focused on the individual, but is hope for the community. It is not about expectations of objectifiable benefits for individuals, nor an anticipation of a predictable future, (which can never be certain even from a philosophical standpoint). Rather, it is a gift from Jesus Christ, who is both now and yet to come, which empowers Christians to live ethically in the present and to face what the future may bring.

5. Conclusions: Consequences for Ethics and Moral Argument

For Barth, hope as a trusting relationship is an orientation to the good beyond oneself. Trust in the good implies commitment to it. This has practical consequences for behaviour. This idea of human situatedness seem to me to fit reasonably with the first premise that is described by Selling in his reading of account of the human person by Thomas. Human persons are created, redeemed and fulfilled by God, and open to Him, whether or not they are aware of it. I have shown as an example that Barth's treatment of hope clearly brings it within the purview of the goal oriented approach described by Selling. Barth's reading of human situatedness calls for interpretation or discernment by each individual as they work out their personal responses to the divine invitation of love, which parallels Selling's conclusions from Thomas on the need for evaluation of circumstances in moral reasoning. Barth identifies effort and struggle in humanity's discernment of the call to the good which is God. Similarly, the moral event, as Selling sees it in Thomas, is impacted by both human freedom to get things wrong, and God's grace in supporting human attempts to get it right.

Overall, these accounts of Thomas and Barth seem to me to be converging on a much more dynamic understanding of how human beings can try to act ethically or morally than the normative rule approaches. Selling offers a better interpretation of what Thomas intended in his discussion of natural law than those following the revival of natural law. The latter have been extensively critiqued; see, for example, McInerny's essay on Grisez and Thomism (McInerny 2000), and indeed, the whole volume edited by Nigel Biggar and Rufus Black (Biggar and Black 2000). Normative rule based approaches to ethics do not seem to recognise the impossibility, after the philosophical critiques of modernity in the last hundred years, of ignoring hermeneutic as an essential component of the human reception of reality. Further, the 'ethical moment' is different in kind from the 'logical moment'. Deductive logic, applied to set rules whose premises must predict the conclusion, admits of no deviation and no doubt, and is the operation of a self-sufficient, independent agent. The 'ethical moment' is the pursuit of the good against odds, and is always a *'kairos'*, a moment of grace in which something beyond the self is given. Such an approach can be nuanced in particular human circumstances, and expanded to meet new ethical questions raised by developments in human activity. It can also be communicated in the public space; for example, secular philosophers such as Levinas (1969) and Ricoeur (1992) provide foundational philosophical accounts of ethics which converge on these theological approaches. David Ford points to this in *Self and Salvation* (Ford 1999, pp. 130–36). This said, such a view of ethics is likely to be challenging to those seeking guidance in a complex and confusing pluralist culture, and effort should be expended on rendering the issues intelligible. Nevertheless, I think a conception which includes a both a hermeneutic and a teleological element is essential to any functional discussion of moral reasoning and ethics, and I claim that such is to be found in both Barth and in Thomas.

Conflicts of Interest: The author declares no conflict of interest.

References

Barth, Karl. 1956–1975. *Church Dogmatics*. Edinburgh: T & T Clark.
Biggar, Nigel. 1993. *The Hastening that Waits: Karl Barth's Ethics*. Oxford: OUP.
Biggar, Nigel. 2010. Karl Barth's Protestant Ethics Revisited. In *Commanding Grace*. Edited by Daniel Migliore. Grand Rapids: Eerdmans, pp. 26–49.
Biggar, Nigel. 2011. *Behaving in Public*. Grand Rapids: Eerdmans.
Biggar, Nigel, and Rufus Black, eds. 2000. *The Revival of Natural Law: Philosophical, Theological and Ethical Responses to the Finnis-Grisez School*. Aldershot: Ashgate.
Bonny, Johan. 2014. Synod on the Family—Expectations of a Diocesan Bishop. September 1. Available online: http://www.associationofcatholicpriests.ie/2014/09/synod-on-the-family-expectations-of-a-diocesan-bishop/ (accessed on 19 April 2017).
Brown, Calum. 2001. *The Death of Christian Britain*. London: Routledge.
Ford, David. 1999. *Self and Salvation: Being Transformed*. Cambridge: CUP.
Hauerwas, Stanley. 2001. *With the Grain of the Universe*. Grand Rapids: Brazos Press.
Hunsinger, George. 1991. *How to Read Karl Barth: The Shape of His Theology*. Oxford: OUP.
Janssens, Louis. 1988. Time and Space in Morals. In *Personalist Morals*. Edited by Joseph A. Selling. Leuven: Peeters, pp. 9–22.
Judt, Tony. 2010. *Ill Fares the Land*. London: Allen Lane.
Levinas, Emmanuel. 1969. *Totality and Infinity*. Pittsburgh: Duquesne University Press.
McDowell, John C. 2006. Karl Barth, Emil Brunner and the Subjectivity of the Object of Christian Hope. *International Journal of Systematic Theology* 8: 26–41. [CrossRef]
McInerny, Ralph. 2000. Grisez and Thomism. In *The Revival of Natural Law: Philosophical, Theological and Ethical Responses to the Finnis-Grisez School*. Edited by Nigel Biggar and Rufus Black. Aldershot: Ashgate, pp. 53–72.
Migliore, Daniel, ed. 2010. *Commanding Grace*. Grand Rapids: Eerdmans.
Moltmann, Jurgen. 1967. *Theology of Hope*. New York: Harper & Row.
Nimmo, Paul. 2010. Barth and the Christian as Ethical Agent: An ontological study of the shape of Christian ethics. In *Commanding Grace*. Edited by Daniel Migliore. Grand Rapids: Eerdmans, pp. 216–38.
Pinckaers, Servais. 2001. *Morality: The Catholic View*. South Bend: St. Augustine's Press.
Rahner, Karl. 1961–1992. The Hermeneutics of Eschatological Assertions. In *Theological Investigations*. London: Darton, Longman & Todd, vol. 4, p. 342.
Ricoeur, Paul. 1992. *Oneself as Another*. Chicago: University of Chicago Press.
Sauter, Gerhard. 1999. Why is Karl Barth's Church Dogmatics not a 'Theology of Hope'? Some Observations on Barth's Understanding of Eschatology. *Scottish Journal of Theology* 52: 407–29. [CrossRef]
Selling, Joseph. 2016. *Reframing Catholic Theological Ethics*. Oxford: Oxford University Press.
Van Geest, Paul, Harm Goris, Carlo Leger, and Mishtooni Bose, eds. 2002. *Aquinas as Authority*'. Leuven: Peeters.
Webster, John. 1995. *Barth's Ethics of Reconciliation*. Cambridge: CUP.
Webster, John. 1998. *Barth's Moral Theology*. Edinburgh: T&T Clarke.
Webster, John. 2000. Introducing Barth. In *The Cambridge Companion to Karl Barth*. Edited by John Webster. Cambridge: Cambridge University Press, pp. 1–16.
Werpehowski, William. 2007. Practical Wisdom and the Integrity of Christian Life. *Journal of the Society of Christian Ethics* 27: 55–72.
Westberg, Daniel. 2015. *Renewing Moral Theology*. Downers Grove: Intervarsity Press.

© 2017 by the author. Licensee MDPI, Basel, Switzerland. This article is an open access article distributed under the terms and conditions of the Creative Commons Attribution (CC BY) license (http://creativecommons.org/licenses/by/4.0/).

Article

Anglican Moral Theology and Ecumenical Dialogue

Peter Sedgwick [1,2]

1 Honorary Research Associate, Cardiff University, Wales CF10 3AT, UK; peter.sedgwick2@btinternet.com
2 Retired Principal, St. Michael's College, Cardiff CF5 2YJ, UK

Received: 18 August 2017; Accepted: 17 September 2017; Published: 20 September 2017

Abstract: This article argues that there has been conflict in Roman Catholic moral theology since the 1960s. This has overshadowed, but not prevented, ecumenical dialogue between the Roman Catholic and Anglican Communions, especially in ethics. Theologians from the Anglican tradition can help both the debate in Roman Catholic moral theology and the ecumenical impasse. The article examines the contributions of Richard Hooker, Jeremy Taylor, and Kenneth Kirk from 1600–1920, in the area of fundamental moral theology.

Keywords: moral theology; ecumenism; Anglican Communion; Roman Catholic Church; moral virtue; Imitation of Christ; moral judgements; moral absolutes; adiaphora/ἀδιάφορα

There are three arguments which I wish to advance in this article. The first is that Roman Catholic moral theology has been in a state of sustained engagement, and sometimes outright conflict, on the nature of moral theology, and the place of the human agent, since the 1960s. This is at the heart of Joseph Selling's recent and very valuable book, *Reframing Catholic Theological Ethics* (Selling 2016). It is this book which was honoured by a conference at Heythrop College, London, in January 2017, both for its own sake and as a way of exploring what the future direction of Catholic theological ethics (or moral theology) might be. I write as an Anglican moral theologian who has long been deeply influenced by Catholic moral theology. It gives me great pleasure to be included in this collection of essays, and to reflect on the ecumenical dialogue in moral theology.[1] That could, of course, include dialogue with the Protestant and Orthodox traditions, but in this case I confine my article to the Anglican-Roman Catholic conversation in the area of ethics. The nature of theological method in ethics remains strongly disputed inside the Catholic moral community.

The second argument of this article is that this debate has overshadowed the search for ecumenical rapprochement in many places, but especially the acceptance of the report on moral theology entitled *Life in Christ* from the Anglican-Roman Catholic International Commission (ARCIC) (Anglican Consultative Council/Pontifical Council for Promoting Christian Unity 1994).[2] The result of this

---

1 Due to personal circumstances I was unable to attend the conference. I am very grateful to the conference organisers that my paper for the conference has been included in the collection of articles from the conference.
2 The author has been an Anglican member of the Anglican-Roman Catholic International Commission (ARCIC III) from 2011–2017, but writes this article in a personal capacity only. At the time of writing (September 2017), the membership of the next phase of ARCIC III, which will begin in 2018, has yet to be announced. ARCIC III has profited from study of, and dialogue with, regional Anglican-Roman Catholic dialogues. The term 'regional' is chosen deliberately as it does not have ecclesiological implications, in the way that for instance 'local' has, which refers to a diocese in Roman Catholic ecclesiology. One such regional dialogue studied by ARCIC III is the Anglican-Roman Catholic Theological Consultation in the USA (ARC USA), and their 2014 publication 'Ecclesiology and Moral Discernment: Seeking a Unified Moral Witness'.
   The present article does not comment on the ARC USA document, but a longer article which included a greater consideration of ecumenical dialogue in moral theology would certainly do so. Likewise, because the focus of the present article is on the understanding of moral norms and judgments in Roman Catholic moral theology, especially the work of Selling, there is no discussion of how Taylor and Kirk's understanding of casuistry can be used to respond to the ARC USA document on the teaching charism of the church. The author of this article will publish (Sedgwick forthcoming) which will contain extensive treatment of casuistry in Taylor's works.

has been a series of parallel discussions. There has been little, or almost no, discussion between the two communions on matters of gender and sexuality. What there has been is extensive discussions on social ethics, especially on the trafficking of peoples and global development.

Thirdly, there are contributions which Anglican ethics can bring both to the Catholic debate, and to ecumenism, in the area of moral norms and the nature of a moral absolute. I will look at three past Anglican theologians, Richard Hooker, Jeremy Taylor, and Kenneth Kirk. I will explore this contribution at length in this article.

It is generally accepted that the publication in 1993 of the Papal encyclical *Veritatis Splendor* was designed to end the dominance of a particular style of moral theology within the Roman Catholic Church. A Papal encyclical clearly has intrinsic authority, but the question is whether it has formulated the issue correctly, and also whether it reflects the guidance of the Spirit. Joseph Selling challenged the centrality of *Veritatis Splendor* for the very understanding of the nature of moral theology. He wrote in an article in the *Heythrop Journal* in 2010:

> Ever since *Veritatis Splendor* laid claim to the idea that the principle factor in determining the morality of human activity was the choice of the object of a human act, I have been intrigued by the challenge that this presents to anyone who is persuaded by the idea that human activity can only be morally evaluated after all the relevant factors have been taken into account ... It is plausible because the entire tradition of the manuals of moral theology maintained that it is primarily the object of human activity, that behaviour which a person performs, that can be sufficient for determining whether or not a sin has been committed ... It is a narrow view of moral discernment because, expressed in this manner, it focuses exclusively upon behaviour without any consideration of the human person as committed to a life project (Selling 2010).

Veritatis Splendor itself is clear on the centrality of the place of the object for a proper construal of moral discernment and moral judgement:

> If the object of the concrete action is not in harmony with the true good of the person, the choice of that action makes our will and ourselves morally evil, thus putting us in conflict with our ultimate end, the supreme good, God himself ... The primary and decisive element for moral judgment is the object of the human act, which establishes whether it is capable of being ordered to the good and to the ultimate end, which is God.[3]

You can contrast the argument of *Veritatis Splendor* with the entry on 'truthfulness' by Waldemar Molinski in the English translation of Karl Rahner's theological encyclopaedia *Sacramentum Mundi*, published in 1970. It showed how Catholic moral theology was changing, at least on the continent of Europe. Molinski wrote:

> Truth is defined primarily as ontological, the basic intelligibility of all things, with God as the first truth. Further, God is held to be knowable but incomprehensible, while man is understood to be a being created in order to know and love God, who finds therefore his true self in being blessed by God and giving himself to God. The main task of an ethics of truth is then to remain as absolutely open for the truth in whatever guise man encounters it, and to unconditionally follow out the known truth in action. The ethics of truth will mainly take the form of an ethics of the disposition, insisting on the formal attitude. Hence an ethics of truth cannot do without reflection on one's personal consciousness and its implications (Molinski 1970).

This understanding of the relationship of the person and truth underlies the foundational shift in 20th century Catholic theology, from the 1950s onwards. It can be analysed into its different parts.

---

[3] *Veritatis Splendor*, para. 73, 79.

How does one measure moral truth? What is meant by the right realisation of the human person? In what way does the love of God, or more simply charity/*caritas*, establish and call the human person? How is this call related to becoming a member of the church that is the community of those who are disciples of Jesus Christ? None of these questions uses the methodology of 'the object of the human act', in the way the traditional manuals of moral theology had done, and which *Veritatis Splendor* was to revive. The questions mentioned above were to preoccupy those who became known as the revisionist moral theologians, and who were most prominent in the 1950s–1960s. Prominent members of this group were Bernard Haring, Josef Fuchs, Louis Janssens, and Alfons Auer. In turn these theologians mentored others, such as James Keenan. The development of moral theology in this direction also provoked a strong reaction, especially from traditional Thomists. This reaction gathered strength from the 1970s, and included those who maintained that their traditional interpretation of Thomas Aquinas was still correct (Russell Hittinger and Ralph McInerny); the new natural law school (Germain Grisez and John Finnis); and those theologians who became leaders of the Roman Catholic Church from the late 1970s (Karol Wojtyla, later Pope John Paul II, and Josef Ratzinger, later Pope Benedict XV). The debate between the followers of what came to be known as the revisionist school, or those who defined themselves as creating an autonomous ethics, and their critics dominated the second half of the 20th century within Catholic moral theology.

So, let me move to the second point of this article. At the same time that the possibility of a revisionist change in moral theology was being debated in Roman Catholic theology and inside the Roman Catholic Church, the Anglican-Roman Catholic International Commission (ARCIC) was being established. It was formally created in 1967, after a meeting between Archbishop Michael Ramsey and Pope Paul VI the previous year. One might have thought that ethics, or moral theology, would have been on the agenda for two reasons. First, as I have mentioned, there was a fundamental change in the nature of Catholic moral theology in the 1960s. Secondly, deep ethical questions divided the Anglican Communion and the Roman Catholic Church. Well before the issues of gender or of sexuality, which tended to rise to prominence in the 1970s and 80s, there was no agreement between the two communions on the nature of marriage, divorce, or—most controversially—contraception within marriage.

Ethics did not, however, appear properly in ARCIC for another 30 years, when *Life in Christ* was published in 1994. Its publication was preceded by *Veritatis Splendor*, which completely overshadowed it. This was for two reasons. *Veritatis Splendor* was a papal encyclical, and thus carried much greater weight than an ARCIC statement. Secondly, *Veritatis Splendor* was directly aimed at the long-running dispute between revisionist moral theologians and their critics within the Roman Catholic Church. *Life in Christ* does discuss absolute moral norms:

> For example, a notable feature of established Roman Catholic moral teaching is its emphasis on the absoluteness of some demands of the moral law and the existence of certain prohibitions to which there are no exceptions. In these instances, what is prohibited is intrinsically disordered and therefore objectively wrong. Anglicans, on the other hand, while acknowledging the same ultimate values, are not persuaded that the laws as we apprehend them are necessarily absolute. In certain circumstances, they would argue, it might be right to incorporate contextual and pastoral considerations in the formulation of a moral law, on the grounds that fundamental moral values are better served if the law sometimes takes into account certain contingencies of nature and history and certain disorders of the human condition.[4]

This was not an approach that was compatible with *Veritatis Splendor*. *Veritatis Splendor* states clearly:

---

[4] *Life in Christ*, para. 52.

Reason attests that there are objects of the human act which are by their nature "incapable of being ordered" to God, because they radically contradict the good of the person made in his image. These are the acts which, in the Church's moral tradition, have been termed "intrinsically evil" (*intrinsece malum*): they are such always and per se, in other words, on account of their very object, and quite apart from the ulterior intentions of the one acting and the circumstances.[5]

Life in Christ has never been considered by the Congregation for the Doctrine of the Faith, and very few bishops' conferences have made statements either—one of the few was the US Catholic Bishops Conference, which called for clarification on the relationship between *Life in Christ* and *Veritatis Splendor*. However, the General Synod of the Church of England did finally debate it in 2009. There was an interesting contribution to the debate by the Archbishop of Canterbury Rowan Williams, under his own name (which is highly unusual for a Synod debate), which sets out some fairly far-reaching criticisms of *Life in Christ*, but also sees it as a document which could be built on. In particular, Rowan Williams looks back to the Anglican, and Protestant, tradition of the 16th and 17th century, beginning with Richard Hooker, but also extending into the 18th century, with Joseph Butler. I will come back to this. He wrote:

> It is not only that Anglican theology developed a quite sophisticated tradition of casuistry (*Life in Christ* 1994, §45): in addition to this essentially pastoral element (exemplified by writers like Jeremy Taylor), there was much discussion of the concept of the laws of God, above all in Richard Hooker, and of the foundations of ethical coherence in the very concept of a creator, as in Bishop Joseph Butler's sermons and systematic works ... This lack of historical perspective explains (though it does not justify) the implication that notions of absolute moral law are somehow foreign to the Anglican ethos (Williams 2009).[6]

It is not clear, however, that Anglican theology has been quite so comfortable with the idea of 'absolute moral law', as we shall see when discussing Hooker and Kirk. It may well be that *Life in Christ* argued its case better than Archbishop Rowan had appreciated. It is clear that there are some actions which are always wrong for any human being (let alone a Christian) to commit, but the issue is how that moral judgement on the absolute wrongness of an action is formulated. I will return to this point in the final part of this article.

In terms of ecumenical dialogue, Archbishop Rowan Williams and Pope Benedict in 2008 finally agreed to restart the ARCIC dialogue, now called ARCIC III, and to focus on two areas. One is the relationship of the local and universal church. The other is to look again at moral decision-making, within an ecclesial context. In the preparatory document of 2008, it drew specific attention to the disagreements within the Anglican Communion. The challenge was therefore issued as to whether there could be an agreement about how Anglican methodology worked in ethics, and whether the Roman Catholic members of ARCIC III could find a way of common ground between that position and their own. ARCIC III began in 2011, and I am one of the Anglican moral theologians on the Commission. This article is, of course, only my personal opinion, and does not commit the Commission in any way.

Now, let me move to the third point of this article. How can Anglican moral theology assist the debate which Joseph Selling's book sets out so well? Selling's book contains a lengthy analysis of Aquinas' *Summa Theolgiae*, I-II, questions 1–21. This passage of the *Summa* concerns the structure of the moral event, including what is voluntary, and what Thomas calls 'circumstances'. Selling argues that in Thomas, 'the moral evaluation of human activity begins with the integrity of moral intention, which is subsequently followed by a consideration of behavioural options. Who one is, the moral character

---

[5] *Veritatis Splendor*, para. 80.
[6] General Synod article 24 June 2009.

that the acting person exhibits, is by far more important than the sometimes clumsy, uninformed, or simply mistaken behavioural choices that we make' (Selling 2016, p. 82).

This emphasis on the virtues, which is central to Selling's argument, is also found in many Anglican theologians, especially the Caroline divines, such as Jeremy Taylor. Taylor, in *The Great Exemplar*, published in 1649 the first life of Christ in the English language. It was an innovation, because it combined a biography with an 'Imitation of Christ', as a book of practical devotion. It was also, and this is relevant to this article, a work on moral theology, where he wrote extensively on the virtues which Christ embodied, and which Christians should follow. The work is Christocentric, based on a strong doctrine of the Spirit, and sets out what a 'life in Christ' might look like. In that way it anticipates the ARCIC document *Life in Christ*. Taylor's work has a much longer full title, which opens with the words 'The Great Exemplar of Sanctity and Holy Life ... in the History of the Life and Death of the ever blessed Jesus Christ.' Taylor's section on the beatitudes includes a consideration of the virtues, including prudence: 'It will require our prudence and care to preserve the simplicity of our purposes and humility of our spirit' (Taylor 1822–1828; McAdoo 1994). The relevance to Selling's emphasis on virtue ethics in his book is clear.

The consideration of moral absolutes by the 16th century Anglican theologian Richard Hooker is also instructive here. Hooker's philosophy of action is opposed to soft and hard determinism, and he believes that the cause of human error in action and belief-formation is because one of the mental faculties has failed to function correctly (Voak 2003).[7] Hooker is different from both Aquinas and Calvin in accepting both liberty of spontaneity and liberty of indifference. Hooker has his own conception of how human beings are able to reason, desire, and imagine. Hooker had a strong commitment to free will both in his discussion of the relationship of will and reason in his philosophy of mind, and in his discussion of sin and wrong action in his philosophy of action (Voak 2003, p. 41). Liberty of spontaneity concerns human wanting. We are free when we act only if we act because we wish to act in this way. That is compatible with determinism: we may have no ability not to act, but we wish to act anyway, because of the attraction of the good on what is created. God, who is perfect goodness, attracts human action. So we are free in our action, even if we may rebel against this attraction of desire. That in essence is the argument of Aquinas. The will for Aquinas was a passive power, and it is the intellect which compares possibilities. Will is therefore a rational appetite or desire in Aquinas.[8] Aquinas saw will as only the material cause of action, while reason is the formal cause (Voak 2003, p. 33).[9] Liberty of spontaneity is compatible with causal determinism, and was a belief held both by Aquinas and Calvin.

Hooker, however, is concerned first with the freedom of choice, before he relates will and reason. It is therefore our experience of choice, or of free will, which is metaphysically the determining factor for Hooker's understanding of the philosophy of mind. This is a voluntarist, or in this case Scotist, understanding of the will as freedom of choice. It involves a commitment to liberty of indifference. We are free only if it is in our power not to do it. Hooker argued that the will is a faculty of intellectual desire and concentrates in Book 1, chapter 7 of the *Lawes* on the freedom of this desire. Hooker begins his argument by discussing the practical reason, then moves on to desire, or the goodness which we conceive is best for us, and then finally asserts the complete freedom of this desire. What is crucial is that 'we so like and desire it'. Choice is the ability 'to will one thing before another'.[10] Will, choice, and desire appear to be synonymous. Desire assumes that one thing is to be preferred before another, and since willing and choice are both acts of desire, then they are identical. The object of desire is that good which is apprehended by reason. Hooker thus has a libertarian definition of will, and contrasts humanity with the action of fire, which has no choice in its actions. 'Will in things tending towards

---

[7] (Voak 2003) Henceforward 'Voak'.
[8] *S.Th* I.85.2.ad3: 'reason relates to many things ... and so will can be moved by any of many things.'
[9] Aquinas, *S.Th*, I.II.13.1.
[10] (Hooker 1977) Henceforward '*Lawes*'. Voak, *Richard Hooker*, p. 51.

any end is termed choice.'[11] Even with the action of reason, and even with the attraction of God as perfect goodness on the reason, nevertheless 'the truth is, that such actions in men having attained to the use of reason are voluntary'.[12] Intellectual desire and freedom of choice are therefore integral to Hooker's definition of will.

So, if we are free in our choosing, how is our choice guided? Like Aquinas, Hooker felt that the study of scripture was something which required careful diligence and much training, but when interpreted appropriately could yield clear and normative guidance. There are matters which can seem 'more obscure, more intricate and hard to be judged of', and so what is needed is long study by theologians—those who 'spende their whole time in the studie of things divine, to the end that in these more doubtfull cases their understanding might be a light to direct others' (Joyce 2012).[13] In discussing whether the 'sentence' of reason is mandatory, permissive, or admonitory, Hooker is clear that reason operates 'setting downe what is good to be done'.[14]

Mandatory forms of the sentence of reason concern action which 'in it selfe is absolutely good or evill', such as the biblical example cited by Hooker from Genesis 39:9, about Joseph, when his master's wife invited him to commit adultery.[15] In this case, 'where the comparison doth stande altogether betweene doing and not doing of one thing which in it selfe is absolutely good or evill', then the choice of actions at this point as a choice between 'the one evill, the other good simply'.[16] It is clear that Hooker accepts the existence of moral absolutes as part of the law of reason, which can be known by everyone. However, this is not premised on the idea of an intrinsically evil act, but because of the absolute nature of the end chosen, which in Genesis 39 is the desire of one person to commit adultery with another. No doubt issues of power, control, and ethnic identity were also involved. For example, Joseph was a Hebrew servant. His master's wife was an Egyptian. Hooker therefore accepts that there are moral absolutes, but (and this is important) he does not frame this discussion in terms of absolute moral law. It is 'the comparison (of the) doing of one thing which in itself is absolutely good or evil'. Two points should be noted. First, a moral judgement must be made for there to be moral absolutes. Secondly, the judgement is about an action ('between doing and not doing of one thing') and not about an absolute moral law. When Hooker talks of moral law, it is in terms of 'the lawe of reason', which 'is that which men by discourse of naturall reason have rightly found out'.[17]

One final point in Hooker should be noted. Actions neither required nor forbidden by the moral law are called morally indifferent. Reason in matters of ἀδιάφορα can only make out a probable case, and Hooker leaves the conclusion of the argument as a matter for the individual Christian conscience. That gives a freedom to consider the possibility of change in matters of order and polity. However, the conscience is always guided by the voice of the Church. Hooker is emphatically not a proto-liberal. Hooker is a conservative, and in most things he feels that longevity carries the benefit of presumption. But just as sins of malice can be caused by vicious customs, especially if they are long established, so too can customs become harmful, even if they were good when established. 'How sometimes that hath done great good, which afterwards when time hath changed the ancient course of things, doth growe to be either very hurtfull, or not so greatly profitable and necessary.'[18]

The answer is then an appeal to the authority of the Church. 'The Church being a body which dyeth not hath always power, as occasion requireth, no less to ordeine that which never was, then to ratifie what hath bene before ... The Church hath authoritie to establish that for an order at one tyme, which at another it maie abolish, and in both it doe well ... Lawes touching matters of order

---

[11] Lawes, 1.78.6 (I.7.2). Voak, Richard Hooker, p. 52.
[12] Lawes, 1.78.31–2. (I.7.3).
[13] (Joyce 2012) Henceforward 'Joyce'. Lawes, 1.13.14–18 Preface 3.2. Aquinas, S.Th, II.II.1.9.
[14] Lawes, 1.89.1 I.8.8. Joyce, Richard Hooker, p. 177.
[15] Lawes, 1.89.5–9 (I.8.8).
[16] Lawes, 1.85. 5–9 (I.8.8.).
[17] Lawes, 1.89-28–31 (I.8.8) and 1.139.3–10. (I.16.5). See Voak, pp. 116, 130.
[18] Lawes, 1,240. 21–24. (III.10.1).

are changeable, by the power of the Church; articles concerning doctrine not so.'[19] The mere fact that a law is given in Scripture proves nothing for him. The crucial question is whether that law should remain in force. Some Jewish ceremonial laws were abolished by the priesthood of Christ; others may need to be changed. So Hooker himself displays his paradox. 'God never ordained anything that could be bettered. Yet many things he hath that have been changed and that for the better. That which succeeds as better now when change is required had been worse when that which now is changed was instituted.'[20]

This is important not only as a challenge to *Veritatis Splendor*, but also in ecumenical dialogue. As an Anglican moral theologian on the Anglican Roman Catholic International Commission, I struggle with the idea of intrinsically evil acts, and this would echo earlier Anglican writers. Bishop Kenneth Kirk, for instance, who was the leading English Anglican ethicist in the early 20th century, argued for 'immutable principles of right and wrong which may be called the perfect law of God', but 'secondary principles are left to man to interpret' (Kirk 1927).[21] These absolutes are predicated of principles, not actions, and the application of authoritative principles is complex and difficult. Kirk was skeptical of ecclesiastical claims to unquestioning obedience, even though he was Bishop of Oxford. 'The Church of this century or that may make a similar claim, and once again the principle on whose behalf the claim is authoritative for those who made it. But none of these factors guarantee eternal immutability.' Kirk accepted that there was 'truth as it exists in the mind of God' which is 'the immutable divine law.' Beyond that there were only variables, and secondary principles of divine law would merge into human law in the ecclesiastical sphere (Kirk 1927, pp. 77–78). This required careful interpretation.

So, let me conclude this article. I have argued three things. First, I agree with Professor Selling that there is indeed an impasse in Roman Catholic methodology in moral theology. *Veritatis Splendor* certainly argues that the decision of the Church's Magisterium 'is preceded and accompanied by the work of interpretation and formulation characteristic of the reason of individual believers and of theological reflection'.[22] However, Peter Baelz (one of the consultants to *Life in Christ*, and a prominent English, Anglican ethicist) pointed out that for this to be true, far more weight needed to be given to the reality of participation in the constitution of the Church as is given to the reality of hierarchy (Baelz 1994, p. 90). Baelz also points out the difficulty of formulating a logically valid status for absolute negative moral precepts, since it is impossible to formulate moral precepts in a way that covers all possible future contingencies. This is Kirk's point, and Baelz amplifies it by arguing that actions which are 'always morally forbidden', or intrinsically wrong, are transparently so to humankind. 'Both the claim to discernment and the claim to demonstration are found wanting.'[23] This is also Hooker's argument in the *Lawes*. Divine law can certainly be of aid to the search of human reason, but nevertheless human nature finds out which human actions are 'to be for ever bound unto' as actions which are wrong.[24]

Secondly, this impasse inside the Roman Catholic Church has gravely impeded Anglican- Roman Catholic ecumenical dialogue. As this dialogue continues afresh at the present (and I write as an individual here, not from the standpoint of the Anglican-Roman Catholic International Commission), the contribution of *Life in Christ* as a document must be recognised and built on. It is difficult to do so if the object of the action is at the centre of the moral judgement, as the way of preserving its objectivity and realism. This is the point made by such distinguished moral theologians as Servais Pinckaers, but it is certainly not a way of arguing in moral theology that is consonant with ecumenical dialogue

---

[19] *Lawes*, 2 38. 4–6; 17–19; 22–23. (V.8.1; V. 8.2).
[20] *Lawes*, 1.243.23 (III.10.5).
[21] (Kirk 1927) citing *S.Th* I, 94, aa, 4, 5.
[22] *Veritatis Splendor*, para. 53.
[23] Ibid., pp. 96–97.
[24] *Lawes*, 1.85. 5–9 (I.8.8.).

(Pinckaers 1999, p. 58). Moral judgements can be both objective and realist in terms of other moral theories, as most Anglican moral theologians would argue. It is a sleight of hand to equate objectivity and realism, which are indeed desirable attributes of a moral judgement, with placing all the emphasis on the object of the action. Evaluating behaviour is not the only way to ensure moral objectivity, but one would not think so from reading *Veritatis Splendor*, or indeed Pinckaers defense of the encyclical. There has to be recognition of other ways of proceeding if ecumenical dialogue in moral theology is to mean anything. That is why ecumenism reached such an impasse in moral theology from 1993 to the present, despite the publication of *Life in Christ*. That document was simply side-lined, to the detriment of ecumenism.

Thirdly, I have looked at two Anglicans, one from the 16th and one from the early 20th century, to resolve the difficulty of absolute moral norms. Neither Hooker nor Kirk wished to deny the gravity of moral evil, and both stressed the severity of sin. Kirk, in fact, struggled to allow artificial contraception as anything but a possibility in exceptional circumstances, until his death in 1954. It would be impossible to regard Hooker or Kirk as theological liberals, to use a deliberately crude analogy. What they do emphasise, however, is that moral theology does not begin with moral absolutes, nor with regarding certain moral 'objects' (or actions) as intrinsically evil. I have tried to show how much richer Hooker's thought is than this. If Roman Catholic moral theology is to continue its vigorous debate in the 21st century, as I am sure it will, then attention to Anglican moral theology will be of great help in this endeavour. Joseph Selling has long been an outstanding contributor to Roman Catholic moral theology, and his valuable book, which the Heythrop Conference recognised, will aid that debate. I hope that my ecumenical suggestion is of assistance to Professor Selling's project, which may be called the 'Reframing of Catholic Theological Ethics'.

Conflicts of Interest: The author declares no conflict of interest.

References

Anglican Consultative Council/Pontifical Council for Promoting Christian Unity. 1994. *Life in Christ. Morals, Communion and the Church*. London: Church House Publishing/Catholic Truth Society.
Baelz, Peter. 1994. An Ecumenical Perspective. In *Veritatis Splendor—A Response*. Edited by Charles Yeats. Norwich: Canterbury Press.
Hooker, Richard. 1977. *Lawes of Ecclesiastical Polity*, Folger Library Edition. 1.78.1. (I.7.2) ed. Cambridge: The Belknap Press of Harvard University Press.
Joyce, Alison Jane. 2012. *Richard Hooker and Anglican Moral Theology*. Oxford: Oxford University Press.
Kirk, Kenneth. 1927. *Conscience and its Problems*. London: Longmans, Green and Co.
McAdoo, Henry. 1994. *First of Its Kind: Jeremy Taylor's Life of Christ*. Norwich: Canterbury Press.
Molinski, Waldemar. 1970. Truthfulness. In *Sacramentum Mundi: An Encyclopaedia of Theology*. London: Burns and Oates.
Pinckaers, S. 1999. An encyclical for the future: Veritatis Splendor. In *Veritatis Splendor and the Renewal of Moral Theology*. Edited by J. Augustine Dinoia. Huntington: Our Sunday Visitor.
Sedgwick, Peter. Forthcoming. *The Origins of Anglican Moral Theology*. Leiden: Brill.
Selling, Joseph. 2010. Looking towards the end: Revisiting Aquinas' teleological ethics. *Heythrop Journal* 51: 388–400. [CrossRef]
Selling, Joseph. 2016. *Reframing Catholic Theological Ethics*. Oxford: Oxford University Press.
Taylor, Jeremy. 1822–1828. The Great Exemplar in Taylor, Jeremy Works. Edited by Heber. London: Longmans, vol. II.
Voak, Nigel. 2003. *Richard Hooker and Reformed Theology: A Study of Reason, Will and Grace*. Oxford: Oxford University Press.
Williams, Rowan. 2009. *Life in Christ*. London: Church House Publishing.

© 2017 by the author. Licensee MDPI, Basel, Switzerland. This article is an open access article distributed under the terms and conditions of the Creative Commons Attribution (CC BY) license (http://creativecommons.org/licenses/by/4.0/).

Article

"My Conscience is Clear" (1 Cor 4:4). The Potential Relevance of Paul's Understanding of Conscience for Today's Fundamental Moral Theology

Marian Machinek

Department for Theology, University of Warmia and Mazury, ul. Hozjusza 15, 11-041 Olsztyn, Poland; marian.machinek@gmail.com

Received: 17 August 2017; Accepted: 21 September 2017; Published: 23 September 2017

Abstract: The objective of this paper is to examine the Pauline understanding of conscience, with the view of gaining an inspiration from it for the contemporary discussion on the foundations of the Christian ethics. The meaning Paul attaches to it depends on the context (mainly in Rom and 1 and 2 Cor), ranging from the personal to the communal one. Conscience holds the secrets of human hearts, evaluates concrete circumstances, and discerns right from wrong. It enjoys special relationship with the Holy Spirit, who gives it credibility. Paul's teaching on conscience extends beyond the personal to the communal. One of the most important inspirations we can draw from him is the one concerning the proper relationship between various members of the ecclesia: those appointed to hold authority, and those supposed to submit to it. How should we balance the communal demands and personal freedom of every baptized member of the community? What is common and what is personal? Despite a multitude of cultural differences and real-life problems in the world of Saint Paul and our own, a careful lecture of his writings may stimulate our debates on the foundations of Christian ethics in a positive way and ensure that they do remain the theological ones.

Keywords: conscience; moral autonomy; Pauline letters; self-awareness; faith; freedom; ecclesiastical community

1. Introduction

The moral and theological analysis of the Pauline meaning of conscience has to confront two difficulties. The first is posed by the central place which conscience occupies in contemporary theological and moral reflection, which may lead to a premature conclusion that it must have been so back in Saint Paul's times as well. We may project our contemporary understanding of conscience back into Paul's writings and see in them something that is not there at all. The second difficulty lies in the fact that there is nothing like a cohesive and well-thought-out teaching on conscience in his epistles. Having said that, however, it would hardly be possible to brush Paul's letters aside in a contemporary discussion on conscience.

Paul's listeners were undoubtedly acquainted with the concept of conscience, present in the popular Stoic philosophy of the day. Paul himself probably borrowed it from there and introduced it into the Christian theological reflection (Bornkamm 1993, p. 142). Out of thirty places in the New Testament in which there appears the noun *syneidesis* (or the verb *synoida*), almost half are found in the genuine Pauline epistles (Lüdemann Gerd 1992a, col. 721–22). He would always use it to explain one or another aspect of moral behaviour, though giving it different meaning to convey different things. Joachim Gnilka traces the development of the Christian understanding of conscience to Paul's writings (Gnilka 1999, p. 314).

In my paper, I shall venture to reconstruct Paul's ideas of conscience. I shall support my endeavour with the relevant texts in his Epistle to the Romans and both Epistles to the Corinthians. After that I shall pursue the question of whether his writings may be considered an inspiration to moral theology today, and—if so—to what extent.

2. Saint Paul on Conscience

Although the concept of conscience did not occupy the central place in Paul's anthropology, it made sufficiently frequent appearances to be acknowledged as a significant one. Though he borrowed it from the popular Hellenistic ethics, he remoulded it into an unmistakably Christian one. The terms *syneidesis/synoida* have at least three distinct meanings to him.

2.1. Moral Self-Awareness

The first meaning was conveyed as moral self-awareness—the capacity to arrive at the moral judgement of the moral event. Gary T. Maedors formulates it as "a (...) capacity (...) to exercise self-critique." (Meadors 1996, pp. 113–15). Paul's assertion: "I know nothing against myself." (1 Cor 4:4) should be correctly rendered as: "My conscience is clear" (Lüdemann Gerd 1992b, col. 739–40).[1] Moral self-awareness means the knowledge of moral principles which one has accepted as his or her own. Such is the meaning of *syneidesis* in the Epistle to Romans 2:14–16 (Longenecker 2016, p. 278). Even though the contemporary exegetes stop short of seeing this passage as an early Christian exposition of the natural law, it is nevertheless rather arresting, in that Paul clearly draws a close parallel between conscience and such weighty anthropological notions as law (*nomos*), nature (*physis*), heart (*kardia*), and thought (*logismos*) (Wolter 2014, p. 216). Paul invokes the image of the tribunal, the courtroom, where man's inner thoughts now accuse him, now excuse him, while he struggles to arrive at a correct moral judgement. Paul seems to say that every human being experiences it as something reaching down to the deepest recesses of his heart, accessible to him alone (verse 16: *ta krypta ton anthropon*).

For Paul, the judgement of his conscience was a matter of primary importance. He held it aloft against his adversaries to refute their questioning the validity of his mission and his moral integrity as the apostle (2 Cor 1:12). Since everyone has conscience, Paul was able to appeal to the conscience of other members of the community (cf. 2 Cor 5:11), and even to "every man's conscience" (2 Cor 4:2) (Lohse 1989, p. 213; Gnilka 1997, p. 207).

Important as it is, though, conscience is not—according to Paul—the autonomic source of the moral judgement. It is not infallible. On the contrary, it needs direction and illumination. It is a witness rather than a judge.

2.2. Witness

This is the second element in Paul's understanding of conscience: conscience as the witness and its testimony as co-witnessing. On two occasions Paul invokes conscience as the co-witness (*summartyrein*), bearing witness *with* someone else (cf. Rom 2:15; 9:1). Ancient tradition viewed conscience as an experience of being split into the active subject and at the same time the scrutineer, the judge. The Greek word *syneidesis* has been rendered into Latin as *conscientia*, which can be translated as *knowing the same*. Eberhard Schockenhoff in his work *Wie gewiss ist das Gewissen?* claims that Paul did not see conscience only as the inner voice, but rather as the "personified and objective representative, standing above one and attesting the veracity of his deeds." (Schockenhoff 2003, p. 91).

For the classical authors, conscience was a rather negative item. It was the prosecution witness, reminding one about his guilt. Saint Paul viewed the matter rather differently. Not infrequently, he took great pleasure in the favourable pronouncements of his conscience. He even boasted of it as the incorruptible judge, giving credence to his conduct (2 Cor 1:12). In his later writings,

---

[1] As in the Translation of the New International Version of the Bible. It is the only place where Paul uses the verb *synoida*.

the expression "good conscience" (*syneidesis agathe*) became almost synonymous with the Christian moral self-awareness. (Schockenhoff 2003, p. 84).

Interestingly, Paul did not acknowledge conscience as the court of final instance, capable of delivering ultimate judgments upon man's deeds. Convinced as he was of acting according to his conscience, he did not shower it with unwarranted and excessive praises. He knew perfectly well that there was such a thing as erroneous conscience, which sometimes may deliver a faulty judgement. Or it may keep silent about one's misbehaviour. But the silence of one's conscience on any given issue, or on something that one has or has not done, is not an acquittal. For the ultimate declaration of guilt or innocence, one must appeal to an altogether different court: "My conscience is clear, but that does not make me innocent. It is the Lord who judges me." (1 Cor 4:4).

2.3. God's Placeholder

The third aspect of conscience, according to St Paul, has to do with faith. Admittedly, nowhere in his writings did Paul identify conscience with the "voice of God", unlike many earlier classical thinkers (for instance, Socrates' *daimonion*), and subsequent Christian writers (like St Augustine). He did not however treat it as a mere natural phenomenon. He recognised a very close association of the conscience with the Holy Spirit (cf. Rom 9:1). Only the connection of *syneidesis* with *pneuma hagion* provides conscience with ultimate credibility (Schockenhoff 2003, p. 83; Fitzmyer 1993, p. 543f). Conscience enables man to match his conduct with his principles. It also confronts him with the requirements of God's law written on his heart (cf. Rom 2:15) (Wilckens 2008, pp. 133–35). For Paul, conscience is—in the words of Eberhard Schockenhoff—God's placeholder (*Platzhalter Gottes*).

The knowledge of salvation in Jesus Christ is a wonderful gift, indeed. It is the gift of freedom. Disagreement over eating of meat sacrificed to idols (1 Cor 8; 10) helped to crystallize the conviction that good and strong conscience, informed by faith, can aid man in ridding himself of his false images of God and his environment. It can also keep reminding him of his Christian obligations and arrest his decline from his high Christian standards. Christians should do what is good (for instance, in social matters) not out of fear or external pressure, but prompted by their moral judgement, informed by faith, and their sense of responsibility before God. Paul styled it as doing it "for conscience sake" (*dia ten syneidesin*—Rom 13:5) (Thrall 1967–1968, p. 124). Though absent from other New Testament writings, it apparently was a fixed phrase for Paul, who used it on several occasions as an expression of deeply felt moral responsibility before God.

After this necessarily brief exposition of the Pauline concept of conscience, I would like to venture a response to the following question:

3. What Does Paul Have to Say about Conscience to Us Today?

It seems not much, at the first glance at least. We know so much more about conscience than he did. After all, two thousand years have passed since his times, and people were thinking and writing about conscience a great deal. We know what importance many eminent thinkers (e.g., St Thomas Aquinas, John Henry Newman) accorded it. We know that some writers dismissed it as the pathogen and destroyer (e.g., Friedrich Nietzsche and, in a certain sense, Sigmund Freud). We know that conscience may allow itself to be enslaved and induced to wage religious wars, or may be persecuted under totalitarian regimes.

Today we are surrounded by the ideas that, ever since the Enlightenment, have been pushing more and more towards the greater recognition of the autonomy of man, proclaiming that in seeking moral good and assessing the moral worth of man's actions all one needs to do is to invoke the opinion of his private conscience. It has become a custom to justify anything in the light of one's particular conscience, as the expression of his private and unapproachable moral responsibility, synonymous with his personal independence. Not infrequently, demands of respect for the judgements of individual conscience have reduced the latter to mere personal opinions and convictions, with no reference to objective moral values. In some cases, even if conscience is respected by society, it is rather as a personal fancy than anything else. Some scholars charge the idea of conscience with too close an association with one or another particular worldview, and for this reason campaign for ruling it out from the ethical discourses altogether.

However, despite the distance of many centuries, we still have a great deal in common with Saint Paul and his audience. First of all, we have the same faith in Jesus Christ. We also have similar experiences of conscience, after all. I think that there are three particular elements of Paul's concept of conscience that may be quite useful to us.

The first element concerns the role of conscience in moral behaviour. Although the idea of conscience occupies an important position in Paul's anthropology, it is not a crucial one. His reflection on conscience stays quite firm within the biblical and Semitic linguistic apparatus (Gnilka 1997, p. 205). However, Paul also makes use of the Greek idea of *syneidesis* and redefines it in the light of "his" Gospel (Rom 2:16). The Apostle invokes his conscience in order to emphasise his sincere intentions and integrity. Unlike our contemporary appeals to conscience, which bring the ideas of autonomy and tolerance to the foreground, Paul does not expect his adversaries to manifest their tolerance, but an ability to recognise the truth and acknowledge it in their consciences (2 Cor 5:11) (Schnackenburg 1988, p. 52).[2] The individual is not secluded in the sanctuary of his conscience, but—as Paul would have it—meets there with a witness confronting him with the demands of the Torah, engraved on his heart. Thanks to the witness of his conscience, man can recognise the moral quality not only of his external acts, but of his inner, undisclosed motives and intentions. Paul would probably agree with our contemporary opinion that individual conscience is the most intimate and binding norm of behaviour. However, it would be impossible to harvest from his letters arguments for the idea of conscience as the highest authority on the moral value of human acts (Hahn and Karrer 1997, pp. 776–77). Paul admits that acting against clear judgement of conscience hurts man's moral integrity. However, he does not revere conscience as man's infallible seat of judgement. Rather, he regards it as an extremely sensitive faculty of the human spirit, which must be nourished and developed. He also knows that this faculty may be neglected and left to wither. In the light of the Pauline epistles it is clear that decisions of conscience must not be regarded as "self-sufficient, absolute and definitive" (cf. 1 Cor 4:4) (Schrage 1982, p. 185).

From there we come to the second element of Paul's concept of conscience. It is the link between conscience and faith. It would be difficult to elucidate Paul's reflection on conscience in our contemporary theological and moral categories and refer to it our idea of autonomy. It would be easier to designate it as the theonomic concept. Granted, the concept of the social heteronomy does not do justice to the Christian vision of conscience. But, one is tempted to ask: does the concept of the idealistic autonomy do? Acting according to one's good conscience and regarding it as the sole repository of what is good and right—does it do justice to the Christian vision of conscience? Can we support it with any evidence from Paul's letters? He often instructs his followers about what "ought to be done" (ta *kathekonta*—Rom 1:28), what "really matters" (ta *diaferonta*—Phil 1:10), what is "proper" (*prepon*—1 Cor 11:13). However, his instructions are not mere appeals to the universally accepted moral standards, or to private assessment. These moral standards become binding for Christians only if they pass the commandment of love (Gnilka 1999, p. 314). Additionally, it is not only about the word of the Gospel as the reference point for the ethical reflection.

For the Christian, the key element in this development is his faith in Christ and his active relationship with Him. Only as the man redeemed is he able to accept the requirements of the Torah to the full, just as Jesus explained them in His ultimate, messianic interpretations of God's commandments (cf. Mt 5:17–20).

---

[2] The plural form (*syneideseis*) in which Paul addresses his readers indicates a strongly held conviction about the universality of the idea of conscience.

In this context, it would be good to recollect two statements of St Paul, heretofore omitted, that are strictly connected with his reflection on conscience, even though they do not contain the word *syneidesis*. The first one is in Rom 14:23: "Everything that is not from a conviction is sin."[3] Though Paul used in this sentence the word "faith" (*pistis*), not "conviction". The latter translation is acceptable and widely used in many modern editions, including the Polish one. The admonition agrees very well with our contemporary moral intuition. It has an interesting history, too, going back to the medieval times, when the word *faith*, represented as *conviction*, was in turn replaced by the word *conscience*, the whole ending up as the following maxim: "Everything that is against conscience is a sin". However, the context in which Paul said it implies that he did not mean just about any strongly held conviction, but the conviction rooted in faith, cleansed by faith, and confirmed by faith. To reach such conviction, Paul encourages examining oneself (*dokimadzein*, or *peiradzein*) (Theobald 1992, p. 77–78).[4] His second admonition, in Rom 12:2, warns against conforming to the pattern of this world (the verb *syschematidzein* means *conforming to the set pattern*). He exhorts his readers to be transformed by the renewing of their minds, so that they may be able to discern and accept God's will.

The criterion of the living faith must be admitted as a significant companion to our contemporary concept of the autonomic conscience. Appeal to faith prevents the otherwise legitimate postulate of autonomy from degeneration into a narrow-minded freedom from every external instruction, and helps to understand it as a continuous task of moulding man's conscience. In this way, Christians may resist the ever more popular styles of living that do not withstand the scrutiny of the Gospel.

It is time to point to the third important element in the Pauline concept of conscience—that is, the ecclesial and communal one. Paul appealed to conscience very frequently during one particular conflict within the community of believers, probably regarded by the interested parties as the conflict of conscience. It was about the disagreement over the propriety of consuming meat previously offered to pagan gods. Paul shares the opinion of the "strong" that because the gods in question are mere figments of imagination, Christians are bound by no restrictions (1 Cor 8:4–8) in this regard. However, the conviction of conscience should not govern their attitude towards the "weak", according to whom eating meat that had been sacrificed to false gods constituted a very serious moral sin. Paul advises taking an altogether different route: love of neighbour, mutual understanding, and seeking what builds the community (Fitzmyer 2008, pp. 330–52; Thiselton 2000, p. 644). He quotes the well-known saying (which Corinthians were probably proud of): I have the right to do anything: (*panta exestin*). He agrees, but adds a qualification: "I have the right to do anything—but not everything is beneficial." "I have the right to do anything—but not everything is constructive" (1 Cor 10:23). "I have the right to do anything—but I will not be mastered by anything" (1 Cor 6:12). Paul directs our attention to the relationship between individual freedom of conscience and moral discernment—informed by faith—and the good of the community of believers.

In the contemporary reflection on conscience—especially in the face of the widespread ethical individualism—we should take into account the pronouncements of the Teaching Authority of the Church and her Tradition. It may be controversial, but it is important. Relationship between individual conscience and the Church and her Tradition is often regarded as nothing more than a relationship between the individual and the institution. Those who advocate this view argue that man may preserve his autonomy intact only if he breaks free of the institution and makes moral decisions all on his own, regarding the latter's opinion merely as advice. The argument cannot be applied to the Christian morality without substantial corrections. Of course, Christians cannot surrender their individual moral responsibility to a community or institution. However, Christian faith, though deeply personal, is nobody's private matter. The communal dimension of the faith is at the very core of

---

[3] As in the Translation of the Holman Christian Standard Bible.
[4] The practice of daily examination of one's conduct was known to the popular Hellenistic ethics, as well as to Judaism, which was influenced by the former; the latter employed it as means of comparing one's conduct with the requirements of the Torah.

Christianity. Apart from individual inspirations, enabling believers to recognise the challenges of the present (*kairos*—Rom 13:11), and awareness of their personal motivations, allowing them to preserve independence in their decision-making (cf. 1 Cor 10:29), we cannot ignore the communal effort of the Church to make her believers worthy of God and the Gospel (1 Thes 2:12; Phil 1:27). It implies not only communal moral judgement and discernment, but also the authoritative decisions about what is and what is not in accord with the moral rules of the Gospel, that is, *typos didachēs* (cf. Rom 6:17), the binding form of life in faith, strictly connected with the Good News about the liberating and transforming power of God.

Paul seemed to maintain a harmony between his moral independency and his obedience to the moral rules dictated by faith. He valued his own moral judgements and knew how to defend it, as in the confrontation with Peter in Antioch (see Gal 2:11–14). However, he was ready to subject his opinions to the judgement of other authorities (Gal 2:2), or invoke his own apostolic mandate to instruct believers and appeal to their conscience (1 Cor 7:25). He did not adhere to the then-accepted forms of letter writing, but would invoke his apostolic authority right in the very first greeting (Lohfink 2016, pp. 327–29). However, he could give up his legitimate right to rule and lay out his arguments in a friendly manner, even beg (cf. Philem 7–10). Had he lived today, his uncompromising stance on his apostolic authority would certainly have made him charged with paternalism and lack of respect for individual autonomy. He was apparently not familiar with the mutual dislike of the freedom of conscience and the voice of authority which is so commonplace today. He did not see any competition between the freedom of the Christian conscience, God's will and His commandments, and apostolic authority. Can we judge that harmony as irrelevant to Christians today and reject it out of hand? Or, should we rather see it as a challenge to unilateralism and overemphasis, which has penetrated so deeply into the moral awareness of the Christians of the 21st century?

It seems that standing up to the globalization and dissemination of moral attitudes and standards is the greatest challenge for today's Christians. It may become a source of valuable inspirations and a kind of *locus theologicus* for the Christian moral reflection. Paul teaches us that the fundamental environment for Christians to learn morality and discern good from evil is the community of believers, living out their faith (Schnackenburg 1988, p. 58). Leaving that environment can only widen the disparity between our Christian faith and life in accordance with the Gospel, and lead us so far astray that we end up bearing false witness in today's world.

4. Conclusions

There is no doubt that many concrete moral admonitions in the Pauline letters are, to a certain extent, conditioned by their historical, psychological, and social circumstances. However, they are also free from some contemporary controversies which can tighten the perspective. A scrutiny of the meaning of conscience and of the ways to make a conscientious assessment in the Pauline letters can be an inspiration in the theological moral discussion about the foundation of a genuine Christian ethics. Despite the limits of the Pauline reflection, it has undoubtedly retained its greatest quality: the ability to put forward the main conditions and moral criteria to adhere to if one wants to claim that his or her moral judgement is indeed the Christian one. The contemporary moral theological reflection must not undoubtfully abstract from the living conditions and remain faithful to the today's believers. However, at the same time it must be faithful to the Gospel and must try to translate their demands in the contemporary world. St. Paul shows the ways to cope with that task.

Conflicts of Interest: The author declares no conflict of interest.

References

Bornkamm, Günther. 1993. *Paulus*, 7th ed. Stuttgart, Berlin and Köln: Kohlhammer.
Fitzmyer, Joseph A. 1993. *Romans. A New Translation with Introduction and Commentary*. New York: Yale University Press.

Fitzmyer, Joseph A. 2008. *First Corinthians. A New Translation with Introduction and Commentary*. New Haven and London: Yale University Press.
Gnilka, Joachim. 1997. *Paulus von Tarsus: Apostel und Zeuge*. Freiburg, Basel and Wien: Herder.
Gnilka, Joachim. 1999. *Die Frühen Christen: Ursprünge und Anfang der Kirche*. Freiburg, Basel and Wien: Herder.
Hahn, Hans Christoph, and Martin Karrer. 1997. Gewissen. In *Theologisches Begriffslexikon zum Neuen Testament*. Edited by Coenen Lothar and Haacker Klaus. Wuppertal and Neukirchen: Neukirchener, vol. 1, pp. 774–80.
Lohfink, Gerhard. 2016. *Im Ringen um Die Vernunft: Reden über Israel, die Kirche und die Europäische Aufklärung*. Freiburg, Basel and Wien: Herder.
Lohse, Eduard. 1989. Die Berufung auf das Gewissen in der paulinischen Ethik. In *Neues Testament und Ethik*. Edited by Merklein Helmut. Freiburg, Basel and Wien: Herder, pp. 207–19.
Longenecker, Richard N. 2016. *The Epistle to the Romans. A Commentary on the Greek Text*. Grand Rapids: Eerdmans.
Lüdemann Gerd, Syneidēsis. 1992a. *Exegetisches Wörterbuch zum Neuen Testament*, 2nd ed. Edited by Balz Horst and Schneider Gerhard. Stuttgart, Berlin and Köln: Kohlhammer, vol. 3, col. 721–25.
Lüdemann Gerd, Synoida. 1992b. *Exegetisches Wörterbuch zum Neuen Testament*, 2nd ed. Edited by Balz Horst and Schneider Gerhard. Stuttgart, Berlin and Köln: Kohlhammer, vol. 3, col. 739–40.
Meadors, Gary T. 1996. Conscience. In *Baker's Evangelical Dictionary of Biblical Theology*. Grand Rapids: Baker Publishing Group, pp. 113–15.
Schnackenburg, Rudolf. 1988. *Die Sittliche Botschaft des Neuen Testaments: Die Urchristlichen Verkündiger*. Freiburg, Basel and Wien: Herder, vol. 2.
Schockenhoff, Eeberhard. 2003. *Wie Gewiss ist Das Gewissen? Eine Ethische Orientierung*. Freiburg, Basel and Wien: Herder.
Schrage, Wolfgang. 1982. *Ethik des Neuen Testamentes*. Göttingen: Vandenhoeck & Ruprecht.
Theobald, M. 1992. *Römerbrief. Kapitel 1-11*. Stuttgart: Katholisches Bibelwerk.
Thiselton, Anthony C. 2000. *The First Epistle to the Corinthians: A commentary on the Greek Text*. Grand Rapids and Cambridge: Eerdmans.
Thrall, Margaret E. 1967–1968. The Pauline Use of Syneidesis. *New Testament Studies* 14: 118–25. [CrossRef]
Wilckens, Ulrich. 2008. *Der Brief an die Römer*, 4th ed. Neukirchen-Vluyn: Neukirchener, Patmos.
Wolter, Michael. 2014. *Der Brief an die Römer, Part 1*. Neukirchen-Vluyn: Neukirchener, Patmos.

© 2017 by the author. Licensee MDPI, Basel, Switzerland. This article is an open access article distributed under the terms and conditions of the Creative Commons Attribution (CC BY) license (http://creativecommons.org/licenses/by/4.0/).

Article

Theocentric Love Ethics

Edward Vacek

Religious Studies, Loyola University New Orleans, New Orleans, LA 70118, USA; evacek@loyno.edu

Received: 17 August 2017; Accepted: 7 October 2017; Published: 11 October 2017

Abstract: Joseph Selling proposes a contemporary revision of natural law ethics, making it more person-centered. Earlier James Gustafson insisted that natural law ethics was too egoist or anthropocentric, so his work proposed theocentrism as a corrective. Richard Gula in turn proposed an ethics that centers on imitating God's relationships. This essay combines the merits of all three with the author's own love-covenant basis for ethics. It contrasts secular and religious ethics, with the latter incorporating cooperation in communion with God. One strand of Aquinas's theology indicates that religious discernment is an affective process of union with God, but the typical ways of describing this union court significant dangers of reducing either God to self or self to God.

Keywords: natural law; personalism; theocentrism; love; secularism; participation; cooperation; communion; identification; discernment

---

"None of us lives for one's self, and no one dies for one's self, for we belong to Christ. If we live, we live for the Lord; and if we die, we die for the Lord. So, whether we live or die, we belong to the Lord". (Rom 14:7)

1. Introduction

As I began my career as a theologian, I was fortunate to have the famous Christian ethicist, James Gustafson, as a colleague. I was deeply influenced by a particular polemic that he, like a modern day Jeremiah, waged against any and all. One time he was asked to address senior faculty members at the University of Chicago on the topic of "Say Something Theological." This erudite author of many books announced he had a one word answer: "God," which he pronounced with a long, drawn out vowel. On other occasions, I witnessed Gustafson becoming red in the face as he argued that Christian ethics had lost its center, namely, God. Gustafson's lamented that, where once we spoke too confidently about our knowledge of God, now we hardly speak about God at all (Gustafson 1984, p. 7).

Gustafson argued, "For theological ethics . . . the first task in order of importance is to establish convictions about God and God's relations to the world" (Gustafson 1984, p. 98). A common Protestant and biblical approach is to view God as Sovereign Commander, an authority whose will we must obey. Likewise one typical Catholic focus is to image God as creator whose wise design we should follow. The first has been central in Divine Command ethics and the second has been central in religious versions of Natural Law ethics (Vacek 1996). Instead, I will explore beginning with God as Lover and Covenant Partner. I develop the radical claims found in 1 John 4: "If we love one another, God lives in us, and his love is perfected in us . . . God is love" (1 Jn 4: 12–16).

Joseph Selling challenges the adequacy of natural law. He proposes "that the new standard for determining this ethical language is the human person, integrally and adequately considered" (Selling 2016, pp. 10, 131, 146; Selling 1999, p. 60). Selling sets down the foundation of ethics in the following way: "What is good is ultimately what is good-for the person and what is evil ultimately is evil-for-the-person, integrally and adequately considered" (Selling 2016, p. 146). By contrast, for Gustafson, "The general answer to the moral question from a theocentric perspective is that "we are to relate ourselves and all things in a manner (or in ways) appropriate to their relations to God"

(Gustafson 1984, pp. 1–2). Richard Gula presents a third view, "Imitating [God's] faithful love which binds the covenant together is the moral imperative for living" (Gula 1989, p. 97). I propose a new standard. The criterion for determining right from wrong is what befits the love covenant we have with God and with one another. The difference between my own view and that of Selling is the centrality of God, and the difference between my view and that Gustafson is the centrality of love (Gustafson 1981, p. 236). I modify Gula's point to insist that we not only imitate God's love, we also participate in God's love. This is theocentric love ethics.

2. Theocentrism

Gustafson's disputatious goal was "to propose an alteration of the egocentric, anthropocentric concern of Christian piety and Christian theology" (Gustafson 1981, p. 110). These are real targets. Moral theologians have, for example, read Genesis 1:28 to claim that all other creatures exist simply for human purposes. Catholic Church teaching, such as in *Populorum Progressio* (Paul VI 1967, pp. 15–16), says "human fulfillment constitutes, as it were, a summary of our duties." Spiritual writers encourage a good relationship with God as a way of attaining our own fulfillment. Likewise our culture promotes "self-maximizers" (Smedes 1983, p. 160).

Our biblical and ecclesial traditions, in contrast, assume and assert that we are "covenant-keepers" (Smedes 1983, p. 160). That means our own human fulfillment is not our primary duty. Jesus says that those who lose their life for his sake will gain their lives. But the life gained is not earthly fulfillment. As Adrian Thatcher writes, "Christology precedes ethics and shapes it." He adds, "Following Jesus is worked out in relation to his sacrificial death on the Cross" (Thatcher 2007, p. 53). Even more expansively, the Biblical tradition invites us to locate ourselves within God's covenantal history. From "In the beginning when God . . . " (Gen 1:1) to "Amen. Come Lord Jesus" (Rev. 22:20), our moral task is to carry out our role within this history. What is ultimately good is not what is good for us, but good for God's ongoing covenant with creation.

Theocentrism is full of theological challenges. For example, the Catholic Church has condemned those who argue that we should love God purely for God's own sake (Denzinger 1957, #1327, 1329, 1331, 1348). To the contrary, Anders Nygren argued that we should not love God at all because such love is so self-centered. Metaphysically grounded theologians such as Aquinas allow for us to center our lives on God, but argue that God's aseity and immutability makes any mutual relationship impossible (Vacek 1994). Even the term "center" is problematic because it obscures God's transcendence, that is, God is not one being—however central—among other beings.

To many people, theocentrism seems superfluous for moral living. We can live our individual lives and we can form groups as if there is no God. As individuals, our goal may be to "find our authentic self." As social beings, we must find our place within our groups and then preserve and develop them. Ordinarily, as Selling notes, our daily moral task is just to deal appropriately with the many different kinds of situations in which we find ourselves. Accepting our "multidimensionality implies de-centring the person, both individually and collectively" (Selling 2016, pp. 156, 167).

Nevertheless, theocentrism additionally demands that our ultimate evolving horizon should be God's kingdom. As covenantal partners we should seek to carry out our role in God's world. We are, of course, ordinarily the person most responsible for developing our own selves and the groups we belong to. But our greatest significance lies in the ways that we make a unique, appropriate contribution to God's project. Needless to say, for most if not all of us, actively centering our lives on God is an ever changing activity. It tends to be episodic. Extending episodes into a consistent pattern is sainthood. Gula aptly describes the ideal of this covenant: "with God as the center of value for us, we need to see all things in their relation to God and to integrate all things into our love of God" (Gula 1989, p. 317).

3. Membership

Christians have often employed the analogy of the Body of Christ, of which each of us is a member. A more contemporary analogy for God's kingdom is that of a corporation, since this allows for greater autonomy of the members. Members are the free source of their own activity, but their activity also belongs to the corporation. Within a large corporation's employee flow chart, each of us is related to everyone else in the firm, though often in highly circuitous and tenuous ways. We are not the center of the corporation, though we may be central in some subgroup. The corporation has a mission that is affected by and affects every member. "Put very generally, the well-being of the whole has to be taken into account not only for the sake of the parts but for the 'system,' and the interactions of the parts greatly affect the whole" (Gustafson 1984, p. 16).

To stretch the analogy a bit further, all of us members have direct as well as mediated access to the head of the corporation. Stretched even further, we are or should be bound by love instead of contracts we have rationally agreed upon. If this or that member leaves the corporation, it continues to exist. Put more generally, participation signals a union in which its members are both independent of and dependent on the union that unites them. Their union both differentiates them and is differentiated by their membership.

Given human limitations such as embodiment, each of us can and often does tend to look upon all else as if we are the center. Nevertheless, we are also able to take up the perspectives of others, and our hearts can feel what other people feel. Each of us can realize that we are not the center of the world, but only a tiny, tiny, tiny part of that world. When we are forgetful of this participation in the lives of other people, we live a shrunken life. Since, by God's grace, we also participate in God, we can, somewhat, see the world from God's perspective. When we are forgetful of our participation in God, the core of a finally meaningful life is hollowed rather than hallowed.

When we take up God's perspective, we realize that the God who is love is concerned for the fulfillment, as much as is finitely possible, of each of us and of the whole and its members. To be creator, redeemer, and sanctifier, God must love each creature and each group of creatures. Of course, the identity of God is not exhausted in these relationships, since God is also related to God and is transcendent to creation. Thus, theocentric love should be directed not only to God in relation to the world but also to God as wholly Other. That participation of God in us and we in God greatly magnifies and alters our role. We are stagehands in God's worldly drama, and that is a great privilege. We are worshipers of the transcendent God, and this is holy mystery.

4. Secular and Religious Living

Selling argues that a "personalist ethics does not have to be religious." But, he adds, "there is no inherent difficulty in introducing religious language into a system that claims an openness to the whole of reality and the ultimate connectedness of every dimension of that reality" (Selling 1999, p. 65). Presumably, Selling does not mean to suggest that we simply add language. Instead, I am arguing, the addition of a reference to God should radically revise the project of ethics and of moral living.

Charles Taylor in his magisterial book, *A Secular Age* (Taylor 2007), has alerted us to the way secularism now does not refer to a battle between theists and atheists. Rather it refers to a relegation of God talk and God belief to the private sphere. Some people go to Church on Sunday and some people go bowling; both are equal, optional, private choices; and their respective value claims are not worth arguing about. In this cultural context, Selling is understandably hesitant to name God, since talk of God tends to drive people away from the conversation (Selling 2016, p. 135). Nevertheless, it is insufficient to appeal only to "our human destiny" or to "being caught up in a project that is universal and greater than any individual imagination" (Selling 2016, pp. 136–37).

As I have noted, we do many, many things in our lives without experiencing any relationship to any ultimate destiny or project. Other animals get along without experiencing these ultimates, and we are animals. Similarly, most of our thinking and loving and willing can take place in biological, psychological, or spiritual (mental) realms without being religious. That is, the reference of these acts is ourselves and aspects of our world, without even tacit reference to God as Horizon or Ground.

We can possess a secular attitude that has solely secular goods. Our secular age contains many people who claim to have no relationship to God. They experience no affection towards God. They do not intend to live consonantly with God. Rather, they simply want to do good (Gustafson 1981, p. 227). Many even do far more good than those who want to be in relationship with God but who, for various reasons, including weakness and sin, do not live out that desire. Nevertheless, it is one thing to be a decent human being and it is another to act intentionally and freely in union with God. Anonymous Christians may de facto contribute to God's mission; but such persons are religious only when they act out of a self-transcendence that intends God. Absent that intentionality, at least in an implicit form, their activity bears no religious merit (Aquinas 1948, [hereinafter ST] II-II.27.7).

Still the inclusion of religious intentionality does make a difference in our lives. Aquinas notes that civic virtue is an imperfect virtue when it does not take place within our affirmation of God. Indeed, Aquinas stipulates that no strictly true virtue is possible without the agent's union with God (ST II-II.23.7). Although Selling rejects the thesis that "ordinary virtue" is perfected by charity (Selling 2016, p. 152), I suggest that the difference that charity makes is that the ordinary virtue becomes part of our personal relationship to God. Just as a solitary walk in the park is different from a walk with a friend, so too our awareness of God's presence changes the meaning of our lives. In this sense, charity perfects the ordinary virtue by making it an aspect of our relationship to God. In this sense, charity is the source of "true" virtue.

In religious experience, we can move from creatures to God and from God to creatures. God and creatures can be experienced simultaneously ("mediated immediacy") or sequentially. Aquinas rightly argued that love for God does not necessarily include love of our neighbor and that love of neighbor or self does not necessarily include love of God (ST II-II.27.8.). Still, love of God inclines us to love ourselves and our neighbors as an enactment of our friendship with God. And love of self and neighbor can incline us to love God.

Love of self and neighbor is sometimes described as loving others for God's sake, and that can be appropriate (ST II-II.23.1 & 25.8). There is, however, a difference between, on the one hand, loving a stranger for God's sake, that is, as a way of pleasing or showing love to God and, on the other hand, loving the stranger in consonance with God's love for the stranger. With the latter, we love in union with God's love, not mainly as a way of affirming God, but as a way of further cooperating with God who loves the stranger through us. Cooperation involves union not replacement. Similarly, there is a difference between, on the one hand, loving our neighbors by affirming their inclination to love God (ST II-II.25.2) and, on the other hand, loving them as actual or potential members of God's covenanted community to which they and we belong.

5. Communion and Cooperation with God

For Aquinas, "the end of all human actions and affections is the love of God, whereby principally we attain to our last end" (ST II-II.27.6). One very strong strand of Aquinas' thought is anthropocentric. (Below I will emphasize a more distinctly Christian strand.) I want to eschew Aquinas's anthropocentrism by changing the last part of that claim to read: whereby principally we cooperate with God in living out our covenant with God and creation. The change is from eros to philia. Loving God as communing with God shifts our intention from our own self to our friendship or covenant with God.

Love does involve a change in ourselves (ST I-II.28.2 & 5), but its primary movement is to unite with the beloved. We share in—sometimes we say we identify with—the beloved and in so doing we ourselves participate in the beloved's dynamism. To use Aquinas's metaphysical language, the beloved's form becomes "the form of the lover." Aquinas then argues that, since "each thing acts according to the demands and needs of its form, which is the principle of action and the rule of operation" (Aquinas 2008, p. 121), we therefore act in accord with the dynamism of the beloved. Thus, when we love God we are animated to participate in the creative, redeeming, and sanctifying power of God. We can and should enter into God's practical life, allowing ourselves to unite with the various activities of God, such as God's creativity, God's forgiveness, and God's love. Aquinas describes this union: "Therefore through love, the lover becomes one with the beloved, which is made the form of the lover" (Aquinas 2008, p. 121). A more contemporary way to make the same claim is that, when we enter the mind and heart and will of God, this union will reshape or wither many of our current loves. This is a process of conversion, growth in holiness, and cooperation.

I agree with Selling that Aquinas's description of this process as an infusion of virtue seems gratuitous (ST II-II.24.3). We can preserve Aquinas's anti-Pelagian point by noting that the experience of love is one of evocation (Jn 6:44). Love for God depends on God's invitation. Like all emotions, love for God cannot be simply willed by us; rather it arises in relating us to its object and is dependent on that object. The distinctive character of our loves depends on the type of object we love. When the "object" is God, we have a religious love. What is distinctive about Judeo-Christian charity is that its "object" is God inviting us into sharing a covenant (ST II-II 23.5). What is distinctive about a specifically Christian charity is our participation in Christ's new covenant.

6. Religious Discernment

Love moves us to know those, including God, whom we love. As Aquinas wrote: "the lover is not satisfied with a superficial apprehension of the beloved, but strives to gain an intimate knowledge of everything pertaining to the beloved" (ST I-II.28.2).

When our loves are in order, they do much the work of ethical discernment. Aquinas notes, "love is a certain harmony of the appetite with that which is apprehended as suitable; while hatred is dissonance of the appetite from that which is apprehended as repugnant and hurtful" (ST I-II.29.1). Thus, harmony or lack of harmony between our affections and God provides the primordial basis for discerning what is to be done and to be avoided.

When we love God with genuine charity, Aquinas argues, there is a certain connaturality between God's affections and our own (ST I-II.62.3). This connaturality is crucial for a properly Christian moral life. It enables us to make judgments in light of God's involvement in our lives and the world (ST II-II.45.4.). Aquinas writes, "Now rectitude of judgment is twofold: first, on account of the perfect use of reason, secondly, on account of a certain connaturality with the matter about which one has to judge." His example is somewhat surprising to our sex-obsessed age. He says that many people have to use reason equipped with a set of norms in order to act chastely. But a virtuously chaste person just feels what is appropriate without reflection. He adds, "Now this sympathy or connaturality for divine things is the result of charity which unites us to God" (ST II-II.45.2). This wisdom born of union with God can "direct us not only in contemplation but also in action" (ST II-II.45.3).

Aquinas argues that, for a Christian, the key to being in concert with God is not primarily reason, but sharing in God's wisdom (ST II-II.24.1). Aquinas adds, however, when this love is enacted in this world, this union with God must then be combined with reason in order to make good practical decisions (ST II-II.27.6). Such decisions are not purely reasonable, nor are they immediately given as part of union with God. Rather they are a product of both. In this, Aquinas offers parallels with St. Ignatius's three modes of discernment (Ignatius 1959).

What happens in discernment is communication (ST II-II.23.1). It is part of charity that we explicitly direct ourselves to God and that we experience the world about us as related to God (ST II-II.26.13). The communication might occur through scripture or tradition, but primarily it is a communication of self—God's self to us and our self to God. As Selling observes, this communication or grace is best understood not as a thing but as the offer and acceptance and enactment of a relationship with God (Selling 2016, p. 90). We can, if we so will, accept God's love, that is, God's desire to be interior to our lives, shaping and forming us (Vacek 2015).

7. Dangers of Identification

In this last section, I need to warn of significant dangers in stressing affective union with God as central and disclosive of our moral obligations. Love, I have argued, is an affective form of participation, of unity-in-difference. Desiring to highlight the union that is distinctive of love, people tend to overlook the way love also preserves and highlights the differences between the lover and the beloved. For example, Aquinas emphasizes union (ST I-II.26.2), but he describes this in a way that makes love of another to be a form of self-love: "looking on his friend as identified with himself" (ST I-II.28.2). He notes that we love others as if they are ourselves, but he forgets to highlight the otherness of the friend or enemy.

There are two common mistakes when difference is obscured by union. In a pious expression, we hear it said that it is God, not our selves, who act. St. Paul writes, "it is no longer I who live, but it is Christ who lives in me" (Gal 2:20). In a contrary expression, humans are all too ready to claim that what is good for them is good for others. "Do to others as you would have them do to you; for this the law and the prophets" (Mt 7:12). Psychologists regularly counsel that one of the mistakes in life is to love another as our self. A year after our marriage, for example, we rudely become aware that our spouses are quite different from us. We often have to affirm in them what we would not and should not affirm in ourselves. The shellfish they enjoy would kill us. In this sense, we are to love our neighbor not as ourselves but as one who is different from ourselves. More to the present theme, we can share in some of God's love and activity, but we are not God and God is not us. God needs us to do what cannot happen without our cooperation, for example, "make love" with our spouse. But God's concerns often and properly are beyond what should be our concerns.

Again, Aquinas argues that love is based on likeness (ST I-II.27.3), and that is true enough. But it is also based on difference; the attraction of the sexes would otherwise not happen. Furthermore, if God loves us, then, other matters being equal, God affirms our freedom and wants us to make our own decisions. Paradoxically, when we center our lives on a covenant with the God who loves us, we enter into a union that can and usually must affirm our own semi-independence or autonomy. Likewise, but more so, we affirm God's otherness. God wills the good of all creation and of God's own self, and thus commonly God's overall will may be incompatible with our appropriate wants or needs. Centering our lives on God may lead to disassociating ourselves from what we reasonably want for ourselves and for others we love. The tragic story of Abram and Isaac explores this possibility. Jesus, who tells his disciples, "I will do whatever you ask in my name" (Jn 14:13), also says, "Father, if you are willing, remove this cup from me; yet, not my will but yours be done" (Lk 22:42).

The problem of justifying self-sacrifice for another further exposes this tension between theocentrism and self-fulfillment. Due perhaps to his Aristotelean background, Aquinas has a difficult time explaining why lovers give their lives for one another. In his view, a friend "does not will the good of his friend more than his own good" (ST I-II.28.3). By contrast, Jesus assures us that friends in fact do this (Jn 15: 13). They sacrifice their lives for the sake of the lives of their friends. Aquinas's explanation that friends may be giving up their bodily life but what they really intend is to choose their own growth in virtue fails to appreciate the hearts of those who have made such sacrifices. In many senses, Jesus did not live a fulfilling life. In contrast to an Aristotlean ethic, Jesus did not focus on his own flourishing. Rather, as Selling well notes, he focused on the reign of God that was aborning in the people around him (Selling 2016, pp. 205–7). Similarly, Gustafson nobly writes: "the reason for self-denying actions is that they serve the ends and purposes in particular circumstances that one (or a community) judges to be consonant with God's purposes" (Gustafson 1984, p. 139). Ordinarily, God's purposes include our own earthly fulfillment, so that fulfillment is one of our chief responsibilities. Still, the basic end of human life is to love God within a covenant with God, not to fulfill oneself. Fulfilling our love covenant with God is the meaning of Christian life. Both self-denial and self-fulfillment may be consonant with that relationship. After loss or death, resurrection, one hopes, will follow.

8. Christocentric Coda

What further specifies *Christian* ethics? Selling rightly answers that we should "be attentive to the teaching and life-example, the lifeways, of the Lord himself" (Selling 2016, p. 200). But more than this is needed. Ethics is Christian when we not only learn from Christ but we love him and in that love begin to love in union with him. We participate in, not just learn from, Christ's life (Thatcher 2007, p. 216). But, again, since our union with Jesus includes difference, we love in our own distinctive way. In fact, Jesus said we will do greater things than he actually did (Jn14:12).

Selling asks, What is theological about theological ethics? (Selling 2016, pp. 45, 200). My answer is love of God. "For, 'In him we live and move and have our being' ... We are God's offspring" (Acts 17:28).

Conflicts of Interest: The author declares no conflict of interest.

References

Aquinas, Thomas. 1948. *Summa Theologica*. 5 vols. Westminster: Christian Classics.
Aquinas, Thomas. 2008. *On Love and Charity: Readings from the "Commentary on the Sentences of Peter Lombard"*. Translated by Peter A. Kwasniewski, Thomas Bolin, and Joseph Bolin. Washington: Catholic University of America.
Denzinger, Heinrich. 1957. *Enchiridion Symbolorum*. Edited by Peter Huenermann. St. Louis: B. Herder.
Gula, Richard. 1989. *Reason Informed by Faith*. New York: Paulist.
Gustafson, James. 1981. *Ethics from a Theocentric Perspective Volume 1*. Chicago: University of Chicago.
Gustafson, James. 1984. *Ethics from a Theocentric Perspective Volume 2*. Chicago: University of Chicago.
Ignatius. 1959. *The Spiritual Exercises of St. Ignatius*. Translated by Louis J. Puhl. Westminster: The Newman Press.
Paul, VI. 1967. *Populorum Progressio*. Available online: http://w2.vatican.va/content/paul-vi/en/encyclicals/documents/hf_p-vi_enc_26031967_populorum.html (accessed on 10 October 2017).
Selling, Joseph. 1999. Is a Personalist Ethic Necessarily Anthropocentric? *Ethical Perspectives* 1: 60–66. [CrossRef]
Selling, Joseph. 2016. *Reframing Catholic Theological Ethics*. Oxford: Oxford University.
Smedes, Lewis. 1983. *Mere Morality: What God Expects from Ordinary People*. Grand Rapids: Eerdmans.
Taylor, Charles. 2007. *Secular Age*. Cambridge: Harvard University.
Thatcher, Adrian. 2007. *Theology and Families*. Malden: Blackwell.
Vacek, Edward. 1994. *Love Human and Divine: The Heart of Christian Ethics*. Washington: Georgetown University.
Vacek, Edward. 1996. Divine-Command, Natural-Law, and Mutual-Love Ethics. *Theological Studies* 57: 633–53. [CrossRef]
Vacek, Edward. 2015. Grace is the Emotion of Love of God. *Journal of Moral Theology* 4, #2: 63–88.

© 2017 by the author. Licensee MDPI, Basel, Switzerland. This article is an open access article distributed under the terms and conditions of the Creative Commons Attribution (CC BY) license (http://creativecommons.org/licenses/by/4.0/).

MDPI AG
St. Alban-Anlage 66
4052 Basel, Switzerland
Tel. +41 61 683 77 34
Fax +41 61 302 89 18
http://www.mdpi.com

Religions Editorial Office
E-mail: religions@mdpi.com
http://www.mdpi.com/journal/religions

www.ingramcontent.com/pod-product-compliance
Lightning Source LLC
Chambersburg PA
CBHW040225040426
42333CB00052B/3373